MAKE YOUR OWN . . .

Wreaths
Cards
Decorations
Tree ornaments
Gifts
Christmas treats
Stocking stuffers
Wrapping paper

From shopping and recycling tips to gift ideas for the hard-to-buy-for friends on your list, *Make Your Own Christmas* is an inspiring source of creativity—to make the holiday more special, more spirited . . . and much less expensive! Bring back the joy of the season with . . .

# MAKE YOUR OWN CHRISTMAS

Most Berkley Books are available at special quantity discounts for bulk purchases for sales promotions, fund-raising or educational use. Special books, or book excerpts, can also be created to fit specific needs.

For details, write or telephone Special Markets, The Berkley Publishing Group, 200 Madison Avenue, New York, New York 10016; (212) 951-8891

# Make Your Own Christmas

✻✻✻✻✻✻✻

## Anne Vaccaro Brady

✻✻✻✻✻✻✻

**BERKLEY BOOKS, NEW YORK**

If you purchased this book without a cover you should be aware that this book is stolen property. It was reported as "unsold and destroyed" to the publisher and neither the author nor the publisher has received any payment for this "stripped book."

MAKE YOUR OWN CHRISTMAS

A Berkley Book / published by arrangement with
the author

PRINTING HISTORY
Berkley edition / November 1995

All rights reserved.
Copyright © 1995 by The Berkley Publishing Group.
This book may not be reproduced in whole or in part,
by mimeograph or any other means, without permission.
For information address:
The Berkley Publishing Group,
200 Madison Avenue, New York, New York 10016.

ISBN: 0-425-15057-7

BERKLEY®
Berkley Books are published by The Berkley Publishing Group,
200 Madison Avenue, New York, New York 10016.
BERKLEY and the "B" design
are trademarks belonging to Berkley Publishing Corporation.

PRINTED IN THE UNITED STATES OF AMERICA

10 9 8 7 6 5 4 3 2 1

For Mom and Dad,
who taught me the true meaning of Christmas

# Contents

**1—Rediscovering the True Spirit of the Holiday**   1

**2—Getting Organized**   5
—Gathering and Preparing Gifts   5
—Baking   11
—Managing Your Money   15
—Making Time   18
—Christmas Cards and Gift Mailings   25
—If You Plan to Entertain   28
—More Helpful Hints   30

**3—All You Need to Know About Holiday Entertaining**   34
—Parties to Give   35
—Planning and Preparing for Your Party   45
—How to Save Time and Money   49
—Creative Ideas for Your Party   53
—Making Your Event a Hit   55

## Contents

**4—Gift-Giving Made Easy** — **58**
- Sharing the Spirit of the Season — 59
- With Your Own Two Hands — 61
- From Your House to Theirs — 64
- Yummy Treats — 68
- Remember This — 72
- Practical, Yet Truly Appreciated — 75
- Heartfelt Gifts — 78
- For the Kids — 80
- For Your Coworkers — 82
- To Satisfy the Hard-to-Buy-For — 85

**5—All the Trimmings** — **90**
- Getting Creative with What's Around the House — 91
- Make Your Own Christmas Cards — 97
- Homemade Ornaments — 100
- Yes, You Can Make These Decorations — 105
- Christmas Cards Are Decorations, Too — 108
- Wrap Your Gifts in These — 111
- Wreaths — 114

**6—Making Recycling a Part of Your Holidays** — **117**
- The Other Lives of Christmas Cards — 118
- A New Look for Old Trimmings — 120
- Save That Wrapping Paper — 124
- New Ideas on Gift Packaging — 127
- Christmas Trees — 131
- And Some Gift Ideas — 132

# Rediscovering the True Spirit of the Holiday

If you're like me, you cringe when you walk into stores the day after Halloween and are faced with all those red and green Christmas decorations before you've even figured out who you'll be sharing Thanksgiving dinner with. It's not that you're a Scrooge. In fact, you love Christmas and everything about it. But every year it seems that more and more of the spirit of the season disappears in those pre-Christmas sales. Instead of saying, "Merry Christmas," you feel like the store clerks should be saying, "Merry Buying." Even your children are caught up in the commercialization, running around showing you the latest bargain prices on video games, CD players, football jerseys, and leather boots.

This book is for all of us who just want to say, "Enough." Who believe that Christmas is more about giving than receiving, spending money moderately rather than with reckless abandon, making our own instead of relying on store-bought. It's for people who may not have a lot of time and money, but who want to feel the warmth of Christmas before the season is over.

## 2  MAKE YOUR OWN CHRISTMAS

Here you will rediscover the Christmas holidays. Remember when you were a kid and your Christmas present to your parents was a pencil holder that you made in school or a piece of paper that said you promised to make breakfast for the family one Saturday morning? Even now you can feel the excitement of giving your folks something that you made and thought of just for them. You can reexperience those feelings with almost everyone on your list by giving presents that carry the true spirit of the season. It's much simpler than you think. So many gifts that bring a broad smile don't require a trip to the mall.

Many of the suggestions in these pages are things you might not have considered gift material, but even one may turn out to be that perfect present you look for every year. There are also ideas on what to pick up in a store—because you can't avoid shopping altogether!

And who would want to? We all like buying some gifts and seeing the holiday store displays, but it's that feeling of "you must buy" that makes most of us crazy. Discount stores can be the worst with their huge signs that blare the low, low prices for things like garland, ornaments, and Christmas cards. Yet, you can even avoid that dreaded shopping trip for decorations and tree trimmings with the ideas in here for making your own and recycling items from one year to the next (which will also get your environmentally conscious kids off your back). Go on, be adventurous, let your creative juices flow. These projects are so easy the whole family can get involved. And who wouldn't mind glancing around their decorated house at Christmas and knowing everyone who lives there had a hand in making it look so good?

Sure, this all takes some planning. But with some forethought you can rid yourself of that "I can't believe it's Christmas Day already" feeling and truly enjoy the holiday. Because this isn't a simple, one-day event like Halloween and Thanksgiving. This truly is a season, and the way to put the most into it and get everything out of it that you want is to be organized.

Remind yourself what this holiday is really all about. That's right, spending time with family and friends, whether it's sharing a meal, singing carols, baking cookies, or just being together. Christmas was never meant to be spent running around shopping malls, checking price tags to make sure you spent enough, buying presents for everyone who might possibly give you a gift, and maxing out your credit cards. So make time for the things that are most important to you about Christmas.

My best friend and I have an annual tradition the day after Thanksgiving. She comes to my house to watch *It's a Wonderful Life* and drink hot chocolate with whipped cream and cinnamon. Even though that Friday can be hectic, with continued family commitments and visits with folks from out-of-town, we always work our schedules to fit in this Christmas kick-off.

Let's be honest. Most of us lead busy lives, and if we don't force ourselves to make the time for Christmas, we can let the season, with all its richness, pass us by. Make the most of the time you do have and you will truly enjoy this Christmas and many others. Who knows? With the hints and suggestions contained in these pages, you might even have the time and energy to give a party!

❄❄❄❄❄❄❄❄❄❄ 2

# Getting Organized

The only way to make it through the holidays is by planning. But if you're anything like me, and the word *organization* makes you wince in pain, this task can seem daunting. Yet even I have learned that the season requires some semblance of order to be enjoyed to its fullest. That means if you want to avoid complaining about a lack of time, money, and gift ideas this year, you, too, must pull it together and get yourself a plan. This chapter will help you to start the holidays off on the right foot, so that by the time the season ends, you won't feel as if it has passed you by.

## Gathering and Preparing Gifts

The biggest chore of the holidays can be the most fun if you give it some forethought. Here are some ideas for enjoying it.

Make your Christmas list early—like at the start of the new year. Then keep it with you, whether in a wallet, pocketbook, or knapsack so you have it with you when you need it, such as when you're shopping. You can pick up gifts all year long, instead of worrying about the last-minute rush. You can carefully choose each present this way, and ultimately you will end up saving money because you will have the time to check around for the best prices on each gift. Who knows—you might hit better sales before the holidays even begin. And when everyone else is running around like crazy, looking for this year's hot item that no store can keep in stock for more than an hour, you will be sitting home with the one you picked up before anyone knew it would be in such demand.

❄

Buy gifts and decorations through school fund-raisers, because most of these programs require preseason ordering, as early as a month or two before the holiday even starts. And by helping out the kids, you share that true spirit of Christmas by supporting a good cause.

❄

Those too-expensive-for-a-souvenir gifts make perfect Christmas presents. And if you carry your Christmas list with you, you can find some unique gifts while on vacation. How many times have you found a good deal on jewelry, perfume, candles, or jams, but couldn't think of whom to buy it for? No more missed opportunities now.

❄

## Getting Organized

At Thanksgiving, if you're sharing the day with family, ask them if they would like to chip in on Christmas gifts this year, particularly for the adults. Decide whose gifts you can do this with. Assign each person or couple the responsibility of picking up a gift for someone else (of course, some phone calls will be necessary during the following week to determine what gifts to buy). Before everyone leaves on Thanksgiving Day, have them write out their Christmas list so you all have some idea of what to buy for these joint gifts.

❄

It never fails. Someone will need to return a present you gave them, which means you must find the receipt. And where are those little pieces of paper? To avoid having to tear apart the house in search of the sales slip for Aunt Mildred's sweater, keep all Christmas gift receipts in one large envelope or clear plastic bag so that you can find them easily, if necessary. This means going through your packages or pockets after each shopping trip to pick out the receipts and then putting them immediately into the assigned container. Otherwise you will forget, and of course that missing receipt will turn out to be the one you actually need. For receipts that don't give item names, write on the back what they're for. Organizing your receipts is also a good way to track how much you are spending and how deep into your budget you've gone.

❄

I have spent a few Christmases trying to remember for whom I bought the picture frames and to whom I planned to give the afternoon tea set. But I found a way to avoid this problem. Instead of crossing off people's names as I buy their gifts, now I mark down what I actually picked up for them next to their name. When it comes time to wrap, I bring out the presents and my list and I know exactly who gets which gift.

❇

No matter how early you write your list and finish your gift getting, there will inevitably be someone you forgot to include. Then you make that late run to the store with all the other crazy shoppers buying anything, usually something much too expensive.

Avoid that problem by gathering up a few small, inexpensive items as you shop for other gifts, like picture frames, gloves, decorated tins of candy, toiletry sets, or photo albums. If you end up not needing them for Christmas, they make ideal presents for birthdays and anniversaries—or you might be able to use them yourself!

❇

For large, hard-to-wrap gifts (the ones that come in plain cardboard boxes but have the price and item name on it), leave the present in its original carton and place decorations over the revealing labels.

❇

## Getting Organized

Buy a large roll of plain packing paper and have the kids decorate it as holiday wrap. Start unrolling the paper over a period of time and let the kids draw all over it a little each day. Then cut it as you would store-bought wrapping paper, sizing it for each gift. If the kids begin the paper decorating early, you can wrap whenever you are ready without waiting for your little artists to complete the entire roll.

❄

If you want to make a donation of food, gifts, or money to a homeless shelter, contact the organization a month or two before the holiday so they can tell you what they need.

If you will be seeking donations from family and friends for a good cause, approach them early, also, while they have the time and money to help.

❄

Check the local paper, as well as church bulletins and store windows, for dates for tag sales, local craft shows, art shows, and school and church bazaars. You will not want to miss these ideal places to find unique gifts for many of the people on your list.

❄

Set a deadline—Thanksgiving would be ideal—when you would like to be finished buying all of your gifts. Sure, a few things will linger past that date, but your later trips to the mall will be much more relaxed than those of most other shoppers.

✻

On your list for whom to buy for, put down at least one or two gift ideas next to each person's name. This way you spend more time shopping and less browsing.

✻

Check your list just before you enter a store so that you can try to get several presents in one trip.

✻

Most stores wrap gifts for free during the holidays. Take advantage of this service to save yourself time wrapping and the expense of buying gift paper. Just make sure to mark in small letters on the wrapping paper who each gift is for so you won't end up having to unwrap any presents before you hand them out. (You can even bring a sheet or two of preaddressed gift tag stickers to the store with you so you can slap them onto the correct boxes right there.)

✻

Ask those you plan on sharing Thanksgiving dinner with to bring their what-I-want-for-Christmas lists with them, to help you with ideas for the few people you have left to buy for. Request that they include

## Getting Organized

clothing sizes. And you can do the same, even making a few copies to pass out to several relatives.

If getting everyone to bring their lists won't work out, then while you are all sitting around the table trying to digest your Thanksgiving dinner, pass out pens and paper and ask everyone to write down what they would like for Christmas. Write up your own, too, while you're at it. It's fun to make out your wish lists together this way, and you can all make Christmas shopping easier on yourselves at the same time.

❄

Shopping is easier if you have a theme in mind for gifts this year. My husband and I find this usually works best for us. Over the years our overall gift themes for various Christmases included books, games, music, and picture frames. I've known other people to give hats, sweaters, and craft show items. By going with a theme, you never set foot in most of the stores in the mall, and you can take your time in the one or two you do end up shopping in. Comb the store carefully so you feel satisfied with your purchases, knowing that you chose the perfect present for each person. And as if that were not enough, there's a good chance you will spend less money this way, too.

### Baking

Keeping this a somewhat relaxed activity takes work and some careful planning, but it can be done.

Baking Christmas cookies, a favorite holiday tradition in almost every house, requires some planning to reach its maximum "fun" potential. This is especially true if this is scheduled as a family event, kids included. So first things first—decide which cookies the crew will be baking. If you make the same selection every year, then this task is already complete. But if your group likes to mix things up each year, then sit everyone down one night at least three weeks before you plan to bake and determine what this year's cookies will be. The simple drop cookies work well when baking with young children. Try to limit your choices to a maximum of six—any more and things, including ingredients, get too complicated. It might be fun to have each person pick out one cookie to make. This can keep the kids more interested in the whole thing, too.

Once you know what you will be making, go through the recipes and create a complete list of all ingredients. Then check through your cabinets to see what you already have and how much. Don't forget to check for the cookie cutters, if you'll be using them. Make a separate list of what you'll need to buy from the store. About two weeks before baking day, or when you do your regular grocery shopping that week, pick up the nonperishable items at the supermarket. (The day before you're ready to bake, buy the perishable foods.)

If your crew, particularly the kids, find mixing dough much less fun than baking or decorating, then make the doughs ahead of time (either a couple of days or up to a week) with just the adults and/or one or two of the older kids. Freeze or refrigerate dough, depending upon the recipe.

Set aside one or two days for the actual baking. Take the doughs out of the refrigerator an hour or two before, unless the recipe specifies otherwise. (Frozen dough will probably need a day to thaw in the refrigerator.) While the dough is warming up, have everyone help pull out baking supplies, like cookie sheets, cookie cutters, a timer, cooling racks, pot holders or mitts, rolling pins, decorations, cookie scoops or teaspoons, a spatula, butter or shortening for greasing the pans, and extra flour to keep dough from sticking to hands.

The kids can help divide the dough, roll it out, make the shapes with cookie cutters, place the dough onto the cookie sheets, and decorate with sprinkles, raisins, colored sugar, etc. But set a rule ahead of time that only Mom and Dad can put the cookies in and take them out of the oven.

While the cookies are baking, set out cooling racks. Then when the cookies come out of the oven and are cooling, decide who will finish decorating each set. (Decorating can be put off for a day or two, as long as the cookies are kept in an airtight container once they are completely cooled.)

Determine, too, which day you will put together batches of cookies for gifts. Before you make up the baskets, plates, etc. have a list of who exactly you plan to give them to, so no one is forgotten. This might be a good time to remember the mail carrier, building superintendent, hairdresser, vet, or baby-sitter.

And when you're all done, pull out some cups and a gallon of milk and get munching!

## 14   MAKE YOUR OWN CHRISTMAS

❄

Finding time to cook as a group is often impossible, with so many busy schedules to accommodate. So try baking cookies with friends or relatives for gift-giving *without* getting together to do the work. Each person makes a large batch of one or two types of cookies. Then everyone passes on a dozen or so of their variety to each of the other bakers. And now you all have a mixed assortment to arrange in baskets or tins to give away.

❄

Before deciding what exactly you'll be baking this year, and before heading to the supermarket to buy the ingredients for the five cookie recipes or batch of quick bread you expect to make, check what you already have in your cupboards. In addition to looking for the basics, like flour and white sugar, see what else is available. Molasses, ground ginger, and ground cinnamon are the key ingredients in gingerbread. You can use bags of nuts, raisins, and dried fruit for breads, muffins, and cookies. The half-full tubes of icing from the last birthday cake you baked are perfect for decorating Christmas cookies. Check also for brown sugar, baking powder, and vanilla extract. If I don't do a thorough search of my cabinets before I shop, I always end up buying another one of these even though I really didn't need it. You'll be amazed how short your baking list will be when you head to the supermarket this year.

If you drew the honor of making Christmas dinner, plan your menu a few weeks in advance. Then realistically figure out which dishes you can make. Assign the remaining courses to those guests who offer to bring something. They will be more than happy to help out, and you can be less harried in your preparations. (When I serve Thanksgiving dinner for twenty-five, I usually ask my mother to bring a second turkey and a vegetable dish or two, and the rest of my guests to bring dessert.) Remember, Christmas is about coming together and sharing, not about being the perfect I-can-do-it-all hostess. Who knows, this year you might even be able to sit, relax, and enjoy dinner with your guests.

## Managing Your Money

You can avoid going broke again this Christmas by following these money-saving tips.

Create a budget for Christmas expenses, including gifts, trimmings, and entertainment. That means going through your who-to-buy-for list and determining how much you can afford to spend on each person—and sticking to your plan. Then decide how much money you will need (and again, can afford to spend) on decorations like the tree, wreaths, new ornaments, garland, candles, etc. If you plan to entertain, develop a budget for food, paper goods, beverages, etc.

Once you have completed your separate budgets, add them together to get your total spending for the season. If this seems reasonable and you know the money will be available to cover it, terrific, you are done. If not, go back and start making cuts—a smaller tree this year, a cocktail party instead of a sit-down dinner, less expensive gifts for some of the people you intended to buy for, homemade rather than store-bought gifts in some cases, etc.

Finding the extra cash for holiday expenses requires some serious planning. A Christmas club savings plan at the bank starts in the fall of the previous year, so you might not be able to use it for this year, but go ahead and get a jump on it for next Christmas. Make some cuts in your usual spending—cut down on one takeout meal a week and put the money you would have spent aside; try brown-bagging lunch a few days a week and again put the money away. And decide whether you can afford to tap your savings plan for some of the extra money. Or, if you know you will have some extra cash right after the New Year, then you can afford to put your purchases on your credit cards knowing you can pay the bill(s) in full come January (make sure the cash is guaranteed to be there before choosing this option—it's hard to enjoy the holiday when you're worried about running up unmanageable debts).

Simply planning your purchases will save you money over last year, because you will not overindulge in any one area the way you might have in Christmases past. And track your budget as you begin buying, to see how you're doing as the season progresses. If you do end up spending more than budgeted for a few people, you might be able to make it up on a gift for someone else or in other purchases.

## Getting Organized 17

❊

In our house we found a painless way to save money by collecting spare change. This works well for a holiday savings plan, too. Here's how it works: Whenever you buy something, never give exact change. Instead, pay only in bills. Then whatever change you receive in coins, set aside. (We keep ours in a large cup on a bedroom dresser.) At the end of each month roll the change and put it away in a safe place or cash it in at the bank. Then put the money away in an envelope designated for Christmas expenses. You will be amazed at how much money you can save this way.

When you're ready to start holiday shopping, turn in some of the change at the bank (or open up the envelope) and begin buying what you need. Or you can give the money you saved as a donation to a favorite charity or to buy food and gifts for a poor family in your area.

❊

Combine Christmas cards with thank-you notes or party invitations to save on paper and stamps. You can put two notes in one envelope, or write an invitation or thank you right inside the Christmas card.

❊

If you tend to rack up the dollars on your credit cards with holiday spending, try limiting yourself to charging all of this year's Christmas purchases on one card. Sometimes knowing that your debt is spread out over several different bills makes it seem you have spent a lot less than you really did. Pick the card with the lowest interest rate in case you cannot pay it all off in one month. Better yet, use a charge card, like American Express, which requires that you pay your bill in full each month.

❈

Check out after-Christmas sales to pick up replacement bulbs for holiday lights, another figurine for your manger, ornaments, new stockings, cards, even wrapping paper. Many of these items sell for half price beginning December 26.

These early purchases will also put you ahead for next year so you can write out cards, wrap gifts, and decorate whenever you are ready.

## Making Time

The hardest thing to find during the holidays is time. Here are some ideas on how to do practically everything you want and need to this Christmas.

Decide early on what is most important to you about the holidays: spending time with family and friends, entertaining, decorating, etc. Then make those events your priorities during the season, and let the others take a back seat. You are practically guaranteed to enjoy the holiday this way.

❈

## Getting Organized

If you plan to give food to a needy family this holiday, pick up what you need during regular trips to the supermarket. Attach a list of what-to-buy to your own list. Have the kids be responsible for putting the nonperishable items in the cart on a shopping trip as early as one month beforehand. Buy anything you missed on your next visit to the grocery store.

Set aside a bag or box for the food in the garage, basement, pantry, or spare room. Then, on delivery day, pack the bag or box in the car, stop at the store for the perishable items, and head over to the church or shelter with your donation.

❅

Fill in your December calendar at the beginning of November starting with the events most important to you. Note any parties you will give or attend, the days you want to buy and set up your tree, when you plan to decorate the house—inside and out (give yourself at least one day for each), when you need to mail your Christmas cards (remember anything sent overseas needs to go earlier), the day you expect to drop off your donations, the kids' Christmas concerts and choir practices, school vacations, any vacation days the adults plan to take, etc.

By marking the special events first, you ensure that you will remember your annual lunch the Saturday before Christmas with your best friend instead of accepting an invitation for a skating party on the same date. And the sooner you know what to expect this holiday, the less stressed you will feel as you go through the season. You might even enjoy Christmas as much as you did when you were a kid.

❋

In October make a list of anything you need to buy this season (excluding gifts), like the tree, a fresh pine wreath, any new trimmings you never found at last year's end-of-season sales, etc. This way you avoid running out at the last minute and will get more done on fewer shopping trips.

❋

Wrapping gifts gets almost anyone into the holiday spirit, unless you're stuck doing it all in one night. To make it a fun part of Christmas this year, wrap gifts over several days or nights. Or try wrapping presents the same day you buy them. If you spread out the days you plan to wrap, you can enlist help from the kids, who are famous for their short attention spans and will cut out on you after putting together only a package or two.

However and whenever you decide to do it, set the right mood, which might make it easier to get the whole family involved. Put on some Christmas music or a holiday video to add to the spirit. Maybe sip some hot chocolate or warm apple cider. This might be a good time to bring out the extra Christmas cookies, too.

❋

## Getting Organized

Place Christmas gifts under the tree in the order in which you expect to hand them out—the first on top and in front; the last on the bottom and to the back. No need to crawl halfway under the tree and lose a few ornaments, a batch of tinsel, and another half hour each time you search for a gift whose exact location is unknown.

Keep gifts to be mailed in a separate place if it gets too crowded under the tree, or if your younger children will try to open them.

❊

No matter how well you plan your season, you will end up with a day or two in which you will try to cram a little extra. For that night, plan on eating a takeout meal that requires minimal cleanup. You will appreciate the extra time.

❊

Set aside an afternoon or evening during the season to read, have hot chocolate, watch holiday shows with your family, listen to Christmas music, or whatever else makes you happy. The holidays can seem less hectic if you make time for yourself, too. And having a chance to do something festive, but relaxing, will make it easier to deal with the demands of the season.

❊

Share baby-sitting duties with a friend or relative so each of you can take turns shopping, wrapping, decorating, or whatever you need to get done without the kids.

❄

If Santa Claus is giving gifts that need assembling, take care of it all before Christmas morning. Otherwise you might end up spending all Christmas Day trying to figure out the directions for assembling a bicycle, doll house, or race car set while your child stands next to you in tears because he or she cannot play with the new toy immediately.

❄

Save some vacation time to use during the holidays. You might want to use one day for shopping, another to spend doing fun things with the family, and/or another simply to relax in the midst of the season.

❄

If you have a packed schedule again this season, consider refusing a party invitation or two, like the one you always enjoy the least. By politely declining, you have found another way to make the holidays more manageable this year.

❄

## Getting Organized

By December 1, set time aside each day, whether it's a half hour or an hour, to take care of holiday tasks, so very few things pile up for the week before Christmas.

❇

Buy all film and batteries for cameras ahead of time. Look for sales on multipacks of film, to get the best price and to avoid running out when you most need your camera.

Purchase batteries for electric toys and gifts when you buy the gift, or make a list of the presents you bought that need batteries and what type they all use. Then make one trip to the store and buy in bulk.

Rechargeable batteries are more expensive for the initial purchase, but they save money and preserve the environment over the long term. And you will not need to run to the store for replacements for another five Christmases.

❇

Pick out Christmas outfits for family members at least two weeks in advance. Have everyone try them on then to allow time to exchange new clothes, find a new outfit, and get dry cleaning completed on time. You don't want everyone rushing around trying to figure out what to wear five minutes before you're all expected for dinner at your parents' house.

❇

If you plan to do lots of shopping in one place at one time, like one full day at the mall, then make periodic trips back to the car to unload your shopping bags. This will prevent you from getting tired and weighted down with heavy packages, which usually causes most of us to cut our shopping trips short.

❄

Keep your camera with you as much as possible throughout the holidays. So many times you will see a great scene to shoot with the video camera, like your children baking with their grandmother or building a snowman with the first snow of the season. Keep your still camera handy also for those family portraits or spontaneous hugs from one of the kids.

❄

Plan your Christmas visit home for a reasonable amount of time. Because no matter how well you get along with your parents/siblings/in-laws, if you stick around too long, things will get stressful simply because everyone is put out of their normal routine, in the midst of the demands of the holiday.

If you find yourself going a little crazy during the visit, do not berate yourself. This is to be expected. Just remind yourself that it's normal and everyone else probably feels some of it, too, and get through the remaining days as best you can.

❄

# Getting Organized

If you just cannot get around to everything you want to by December 25, extend the season another twelve days, to January 6, better known as Little Christmas. This can be a nice day to exchange gifts with friends, give a family member the one gift you could not find by Christmas Day, or throw a dinner party for friends.

## Christmas Cards and Gift Mailings

Sharing your good wishes for the season can be fun if you plan it right.

In November go through your address book and create a list of who to send Christmas cards to this year. In addition to the complete mailing address (don't forget apartment numbers), include the names of all family members so you know how to address the inside of the card. Make a separate list for cards that go to folks living outside the country, which will have to be mailed at least two weeks earlier (check with your local post office for the particular countries you will be mailing to).

If you own a computer, or have access to one, create and save this list on a disk. Then next year (or throughout the year) update it with new people and addresses. If your list is handwritten, make a copy and file it in a spot you will remember so you have it for next year.

✻

For gifts you plan to mail, have them sent straight from the store where you purchase them or the catalog company you order from. It may save you a little money, but, more important, it will save you time and practically guarantee the presents will arrive by Christmas. The store or catalog should have gift tags that go in the package so your recipients know who sent the present.

❄

Planning to include pictures of yourselves and/or the kids in the Christmas cards? Then head over to the photo studio well before Thanksgiving to avoid the long lines and even longer wait. You know the kids will want to be in and out as quickly as possible.

With your pictures in hand early on, you should have no trouble meeting that early December deadline for ordering holiday picture postcards, which you can get very cheap from most film developers.

If the professional portrait routine is not your thing, then simply flip through your vacation shots to find a good family picture to use for this year's postcard.

❄

Set a date when you expect (or would like) to have all the cards ready to mail. Decide how many you can realistically write each night, even three or five each day is good. Then track backward from your mailing date to determine how many days you will need to write out all the cards. Give yourself a couple of extra days in case you miss a night or two. Just remember to check your calendar so you remember when to start writing.

❄

If you expect to make your own Christmas cards—whether drawing, designing on the computer, or embroidering them—figure out how long the work will take you. You don't want to run out of time or find yourself pulling an all-nighter the week before Christmas to finish them.

❄

Remember to check the return addresses on all the cards you receive and note anyone who has moved. This keeps your Christmas list and address book updated. And remember to add those folks who sent you a card but are not currently on your list.

❄

Before you head out to the store to buy ready-made cards or the materials to make your own, figure out how many cards you actually intend to mail. Check your list to get an exact count, then add at least five more to that number to allow for mistakes and a forgotten friend or relative.

❄

When deciding whom to send Christmas cards to, use the practical rule of thumb: only mail to the people you know you will not see for the holidays.

## If You Plan to Entertain

The secret to a successful holiday event is advanced planning. Try these ideas.

Keep a pad of paper handy at all times, maybe on the refrigerator, just for the party. This way you can add the names of other guests to invite, food to buy, dishes to serve, supplies to pick up, etc. Trying to keep all those things in your head as they come to mind will make you crazy and assure that you will forget something.

❄

Assign cleanup duties to each family member for parties or decorating events so that no one person feels overburdened by what should be a fun time. If everyone knows ahead of time what he or she is responsible for, there will be less complaining and procrastinating when cleanup time comes along.

❄

Though most of us feel bad letting guests help prepare or clean up for a party, it really can make things much more manageable and give you the energy you need to get through and even enjoy the party. So this year say "yes—thanks!" when someone asks if they can help.

❄

You give a party every year, but no matter how well you plan, it always leaves you wiped. So skip the entertaining this year. See if it makes things any easier. You can always do it again next year if you really miss it.

❄

Set up for a party as early as possible to give you plenty of time to check lists for forgotten items. The sooner you set up, the more energy you'll have when your guests arrive.

❄

Don't get obsessed with housekeeping during the holiday season. Use the time you would have spent on heavy cleaning doing fun things instead.

❄

If Christmas Day dinner is at your house this year, make a schedule for the day that includes time to open gifts with the kids before anyone arrives and to exchange presents with your friends. Try to avoid quarantining yourself in the kitchen.

❄

At least two weeks before your event, clear extra space in your refrigerator by using up leftovers, rearranging items more efficiently, and taking out anything that does not really need to be refrigerated. This way you have room for your make-ahead items as they are ready.

**More Helpful Hints**

Here are some other ways to get organized for the holidays.

Before you head out to start your "Christmas shopping," check around the house for any presents you may have bought earlier in the year. Sometimes secret hiding places are so good that we forget about the gifts we stash in them.

❄

If you're having houseguests for the holidays, get flight information and anticipated arrival times for those driving in as early as possible—no later than the week before their expected due date. Mark all the details on your calendar and decide who will do the airport run (or runs), who will be home to greet the guests driving in, etc.

Then figure out in advance who will sleep where. Be practical when assigning rooms—the most comfortable bed goes to the oldest guest or anyone with back trouble; kids can always sleep on the floor in sleeping bags; and it might work best for everyone if all the kids share one room if they are about the same age.

Set aside guest sheets and towels a few days before they arrive. You want to avoid making beds and finishing up the laundry as your travelers are walking in the door. Get grocery and any other shopping finished earlier in the week, too. You want as much time visiting with your guests as possible.

Be flexible in your meal and restaurant selection. Plan home-cooked meals that can be served any time in case your guests decide one night to take you out to dinner instead of having you serve up another meal for them.

And relax. Remember, your guests are here to visit and celebrate the holidays with you—they're not expecting five-star hotel service.

❋

Assign household chores and holiday preparation to all members of your family who are old enough to handle the responsibility. If no one seems motivated to help out, develop some type of reward system—for example, everyone who participates gets a night at the movies after the holidays.

❋

Pick up holiday items for yourself when traveling, like an ornament. Most travel spots have a variety of ornaments for sale which will bring back memories of your various trips when you are decorating in December.

❄

If you do catalog shopping by phone, write out all the information you need to place your order on a piece of paper or the order form from inside the book. Then right after you place the order, mark down the day and time on that same information sheet, along with the expected delivery date, and the order number, if you receive one. As your packages arrive, mark the arrival date on the sheet and file the piece of paper with your other holiday receipts. This way you will have your own records handy if there are any problems, and you can double check your credit card bills for these purchases.

❄

When you buy your Christmas tree this year, pick up one of those big plastic tree bags at the same time. Place it under the stand when you set up your pine and when the season is over, pull up the sides around the branches (remove the stand first) and haul it out of the house. Maybe this July you won't find any spare pine needles in the rug.

❄

Pack items you buy at post-holiday sales in the Christmas boxes with the other decorations that you store in the attic, basement, spare room, or garage. Otherwise you might forget about them the following year.

## Getting Organized

❄

The holidays are so much about tradition. And these rituals that families carry on year after year are what make the season so special for all of us. So develop and maintain some of your own with your family, whether it's who you share Christmas dinner with, when you open your presents from each other, which movie you watch on Christmas Eve, or setting aside a day during the season just for your immediate family. It's special events like these that your children will remember most about the Christmas season.

❄

Keep reminding yourself that no matter how well you plan, arrange, and organize, something will go wrong during the holidays (probably through no fault of your own). A visit home or a party can be disappointing if you expect too much from it. So think realistically when planning these events, so your letdowns are kept to a minimum.

✳✳✳✳✳✳✳✳✳ 3

# All You Need to Know About Holiday Entertaining

Along with the Christmas holidays comes the opportunity for party-giving and partygoing. Sure, it's easier just to mark your calendar with other people's social events than to plan and give your own. But in this chapter you'll find ideas for entertaining to suit your schedule and budget. A Christmas party doesn't have any special requirements other than that it happens during the season, which can start as early as the day after Thanksgiving and end as late as twelve days after Christmas.

Remember, you give a party so you can spend time with friends and family. Don't worry about impressing people or making your event bigger than anyone else's. Throwing a terrific party has nothing to do with what is served, and everything to do with the people, the conversation, and the mood the party givers set. Giving your own should not be something to stress out about, but something to look forward to! With the planning tips presented here, you can pull off your event and still have the energy to enjoy it.

## Parties to Give

Maybe you've shied away from throwing a party because you couldn't think of anything to make yours different from everyone else's. Here are plenty of ideas for making yours something special.

This party is guaranteed to put everyone in the spirit of the season. If one of your favorite parts of the holiday is trimming the tree, invite friends over to string the popcorn and cranberries. Before your guests arrive, haul in the tree and bring down the ornaments and lights from the attic. Heat up the apple cider and set out some munchies, like chips, Christmas cookies, crackers, even a holiday cake or two. And when your doorbell starts ringing, put on some Christmas carols or run a tape of *It's A Wonderful Life* through the VCR. What better way to spend a Sunday afternoon in December?

Giving this party requires minimal work on your part, because you're simply turning an annual holiday event into a reason to entertain. Your guests will appreciate the laid back, relaxed atmosphere of your party, where they only need to help as much as they like. It's practically no work for anyone, and fun all the way around.

❄

Not all parties must fall on a Saturday evening. How about serving up breakfast after midnight mass? At about 2 A.M. you can offer the first chance for everyone (yes, even kids) to wish each other a Merry

Christmas. This early breakfast tradition has been in my husband's family for over seventy years and makes our holiday extra special. In addition to family, all of us invite some of our friends. It works out especially well with friends who come in from out of town and are spending Christmas Day with relatives. We have an opportunity to visit with them during their only free time of the holidays.

And the breakfast menu is so simple. Ask your guests to bring breads, rolls, pastries, and cookies, and you take care of cooking the eggs, bacon, sausage, waffles, or whatever you're all in the mood for. Or you can pile everyone in the kitchen as assistants to the chef.

If breakfast in the wee hours is too early for you, then invite some folks over to your house late Christmas morning, after you and the kids have opened up all your presents, but before anyone's headed out to dinner. You can go for a simple Continental style breakfast, which means no cooking, just some rolls and pastries that you can pick up the day before. Or whip up omelets and cinnamon buns if the feeling strikes. Of course, it's easier to serve the first meal of the day when you won't be entertaining anyone later.

We also share a tradition with one of our friends in which we go to her house for breakfast the day *after* Christmas and exchange our presents. Our kids love it because it extends the holiday for them, and her gifts don't get lost in the Christmas Day overload. We keep the food simple—bagels and doughnuts usually suffice. Then we relax and spend the rest of the morning talking and playing with the kids.

Breakfast also works well on New Year's Eve, any

If cookies are more your thing, invite kids and their parents over for a cookie-baking party. Each family brings their favorite recipe and the necessary ingredients. You supply the cookie sheets, kitchen, oven, and other tools of the trade. (But guests should bring any special baking supplies their recipe requires.) To avoid duplicate recipes, ask everyone ahead of time what they'll be baking, because the larger the variety, the more fun cookie eating will be.

Plan out work areas ahead of time for each family so you guarantee everyone will have plenty of room. Set aside cookie tins or plastic containers to fill with a mixture of the leftovers that each family can take home with them. You can forget about supplying food because everyone will pig out on the cookies once they're baked. Just be sure to load up on the milk.

❄

How many times have you watched a holiday TV show or movie and wondered why no one in real life goes caroling through their neighborhood? This year get your friends and relatives together to stroll through your town spreading the sounds of the season. If you feel hesitant about roaming through streets where you know no one, then stop in front of the houses of your parents, your friends who couldn't get a baby-sitter, an elderly friend, etc. Call them up ahead of time to make sure they'll be home. Just think of the warm reception you'll get.

Pick up songbooks at bookstores, department stores, or holiday or record shops (a pitch pipe is a good purchase, too). Pass out the songbooks a few days before your musical night so that the carolers can decide what they'll be singing and refresh their memories on all the lyrics. (If you have any concerns about how it'll sound, get together once or twice to practice before the big night—but remember, it's a celebration, not an audition, so don't worry about it too much. That's the miracle of singing in a group—everyone's voice sounds better!) Arrange for everyone to meet at your house at a specific time and then get caroling.

Stroll along in such a way that you'll end up back at your house for folks to warm up with hot chocolate and cookies, and even a bit more singing.

❄

Christmas Eve dinner has turned into a very special event in our house over the last few years. For most families, including ours, it means serving a traditional meal of ethnic foods from their heritage. Italian families like mine usually eat up to seven different types of fish. Other cultures serve their own unique meals. But if you can't get together with your family for this special dinner this year, make it for your friends.

Send out invitations that include your menu and a short explanation about the history of this particular meal in your family. Most of the people who now come to our Christmas Eve dinner aren't even of Italian descent.

And there's no real extra work involved, because you were planning to cook all of this anyway. Now all you're doing is doubling or tripling your recipes. You don't even have to find a separate day in the season for this holiday dinner party.

But if this seems like it will turn into more work than you can handle, ask everyone to bring a dish they traditionally serve on Christmas Eve with their families. This way everyone shares a part of their culture, and the meal and its sense of tradition becomes even more interesting.

❊

Wrapping presents always puts me in the holiday spirit, but it loses its excitement when I don't plan well and end up rushing to do it all in those last few days before Christmas. (Worse yet is when I get stuck doing it all alone because my husband, who loves Christmas, hates wrapping.) This year invite some friends over to do their wrapping with you—they bring their own presents and wrapping supplies. (Of course, everyone's gifts for each other should be left home—you don't want to spoil the surprise!)

If you know the kids will get in the way with this project, and if you'd like some time alone with your friends, maybe you can make arrangements to keep the children busy and out of the house.

You can keep your little event inexpensive and make for an easy cleanup by serving just snack food or coffee and dessert. Put on some holiday music, enjoy each other's company, and you'll have a successful Christmas party.

To make this event work, you and everyone else must purchase all your gifts (or most of them) in time for the party. So it also provides you with motivation to get through your shopping list early this year. You can try to finish all your wrapping in this one night, but that might be expecting too much. The idea is to get through the bulk of it and have a good time with your friends while you're doing it. And who knows, by seeing everyone else's gift selections, you might even pick up some ideas for the few hard-to-buy-for folks left on your list.

❄

You want to give a Christmas dinner party, but you know you just don't have the time to cook an elaborate meal for a large group. Instead of handling all the work yourself, ask guests to share it with you. You provide the place for the party as well as the table settings, and even a course or two, but everyone shares in the rest of the cooking. You decide the menu and each guest can pick what they will make. This also works out great for the fussy guest or two, or those on special diets, who can bring something to suit their own taste.

Of course, you can throw a similar party a week after New Year's Day. Offer up a casual potluck dinner with some family and friends where everyone brings a dinner dish or dessert. This is a quiet but fun way to end a hectic season, and you can even use this as a replacement for exchanging gifts with your friends.

❄

## All You Need to Know About Entertaining 43

If you're not cooking Christmas dinner for your family this year, but wish you were, then serve up a pre-holiday dinner for your close friends. Make it at least two weeks before so there's some distance between this meal and the holiday dinner your friends will be eating with their families. Plan to exchange presents at dinner, too, and start the gift-giving early.

This dinner party is an especially good idea if you won't be around for the holidays because of travel plans, or if your friends will be heading out of town, too.

※

You can avoid the pre-party set up and post-party cleanup by hosting your event at the local skating rink. If your town has a public outdoor rink—the best kind for getting everyone in the Christmas spirit—call the parks and recreation department to find out about how you can get it all to yourselves for a few hours.

You can also try to rent a private indoor rink. If the fee runs too high for your budget, then ask guests to chip in on the cost, or just meet up with everyone at the rink when it's open to the public. You can pay all the guests' admission fees or they can cover their own.

Wherever you have it, you'll need the snack bar open, too. Compare the cost of guests paying for their own snacks versus you picking up the tab for a limited or unlimited selection.

To keep the kids busy when they get bored or cold, and for anyone who shows up with no plans to skate, make sure video games and/or a pool table are available at the indoor rink.

❄

Throwing a party can be expensive and time-consuming, but you can make it easier on yourself by giving it with a friend. You split the costs and the work. Choose a cohost with whom you share lots of friends so your guest list remains virtually the same, otherwise you'll lose out on the money savings. It worked out great for us when we still lived in an apartment and threw a party with our friends who owned their own house. Because they had more room (and more parking) and kids (we didn't yet), their place turned out to be better suited for the party than ours.

Instead of splitting all the work equally, have each host do what he or she is best at. The better cook, or the one who likes to bake, plays chef for the night. The organizer takes care of planning the party and setting up. This way no one ends up taxed by the amount or type of work he or she has to do. Just remember, everyone cleans up, and the extra helping hands will make it go a lot quicker.

When it's all done, you'll have saved a day by giving and going to two parties at the same time, leaving you with more energy to get through the rest of the season.

❄

One of my many favorite parts of the holiday season is watching Christmas movies. If you and some friends feel the same way, get together for Movie Night. Rent or buy the videos you all want to watch and have a Christmas film festival in your own house. Movies I try not to miss are *The Bishop's Wife, It's A Wonderful Life, A Christmas Carol* (the 1938 or 1951 black-and-white versions, of course), *The Man in the Santa Claus Suit, Miracle on 34th Street,* and *Holiday Inn.* You can include the kids for a little while early on with *The Muppet Christmas Carol, Dr. Seuss: The Grinch Who Stole Christmas,* or *Mr. Magoo's Christmas Carol.*

Pop up plenty of popcorn, serve up hot and cold drinks, dim the lights, and you're ready to go.

## Planning and Preparing for Your Party

The key to surviving your own party is good planning. Here's a schedule to help you organize yourself for the standard having-guests-at-your-house-for-some-food-and-drinks-type event:

*Three to Four Weeks Before the Party:*
* Mail invitations or make calls to invite your guests. This way they can schedule your party before their holiday calendar is filled with other commitments.

*Two Weeks Before:*
* Plan your menu.
* Make a list of everything you'll need for the party, from folding chairs to food. As you buy and get

what you need, check it off the list. (But don't throw the list out when you're done—it's a great reminder of the things you need to use and put out on the day of the party.)
* Buy nonperishable food items like chips, nuts, frozen foods, drinks.

*One Week Before:*
* Make dishes you can freeze.
* Buy paper and plastic items.
* Begin cleaning the house. (Don't make yourself crazy with this one. Most people won't be doing the white glove test.)

*Two to Three Days Before:*
* Buy perishable foods like meats, breads, fresh vegetables, and fruit.
* Finish house cleaning.
* Start rearranging furniture.
* Check that you have the music or videos you want to run during the party. Call and ask guests to bring some of theirs.

*One Day Before:*
* Check that you have enough ice. Buy or make what you need.
* Take frozen bake-aheads out of freezer and place in the refrigerator to thaw.
* Set up tables and chairs.
* Refrigerate drinks.
* Put out supplies to check and see if you missed anything.
* Clear coat closet and add extra hangers. (Remem-

## All You Need to Know About Entertaining

ber, you can always throw coats on the bed if you're tight for space.)
* Do any last-minute shopping.

*Day of the Party:*
* Finish setting up.
* Make and prepare last-minute food, cleaning up as you go along.
* Run and empty dishwasher.
* Rest before the guests arrive.

Here are some other things to keep in mind that might help you pull off your event and make everything go smoothly.

Be sure to stock up on nonalcoholic drinks, too. Besides soda, pick up seltzer, plain or flavored, which can also be used as a mixer; juices like cranberry, pineapple, and orange, which work well alone or mixed with seltzer or alcohol; and mineral water (only if you know someone who actually drinks it). And consider making a nonalcoholic punch to complement the spiked version.

❄

Label refrigerated food containers so you know what's in each one. Then post a list on your refrigerator of everything you plan to serve in the order you'll be using it so nothing ends up forgotten. Leave a pen nearby so you can cross off each item as you take it out.

❄

Organize your refrigerator for the party. Anything that needs to be heated early on or served first belongs in easy view. So put dessert and main-course items to the back, if you are planning a sit-down dinner. Place hors d'oeuvres and dips up front, within easy reach. No matter what type of party you're giving, you can avoid having to spend time rearranging everything in the fridge all night, or forgetting to serve something hidden in the back of a shelf.

❄

Rearrange your furniture and consider moving some of the smaller pieces out of the main party rooms to make more space. You want to give your guests the opportunity to move around freely without tripping over magazine racks, CD crates, and footstools, or bumping into chairs and end tables. This also allows you room for the additional chairs you'll need to set up.

❄

If you have kids who are old enough to pitch in, assign each member of the family a room or two to clean so no one is stuck doing it all. Set a day or two aside when everyone must do his or her work so that the house is ready in time.

Use the same crew to set up and clean up, too. Make a list of what will need to be done, and have family members sign up for what they want to do. Obviously you'll want to make sure the task is age-appropriate and that no one is given more than he or she can handle.

## How to Save Time and Money

You can throw a party even on a tight budget. And you don't need weeks to get everything all together. Here's how.

Think twice before heading out to the video or record store to stock up on holiday music or movies. Call some of your guests and ask them to bring a few of their favorites along. Remind them to label their boxes so no one goes home with the wrong tape.

❊

To avoid overloading yourself, ask guests to bring food, serving dishes, after-dinner mints, dessert, a coffee urn, or whatever. Most people want to help out in some way, and your friends and relatives will be more than happy to bring whatever you need. And then all your guests can feel they contributed to the good time. (Besides, most people will feel obligated not to show up empty-handed anyway, and if you don't tell them what you need, you'll probably just end up with twenty-seven desserts or sixteen bottles of wine.)

❊

Instead of buying a long holiday tablecloth for the buffet table, use a white, green, or red sheet, which is also very easy to wash later on. You can even decorate it in Christmas designs with acrylic paint to make it look more festive. (With a full-, queen-, or king-size sheet, you'll need to fold it in half widthwise to avoid draping the floor as well as the table.)

❊

Borrow good tablecloths, napkins, serving platters, etc., from friends and relatives instead of buying new ones. Also borrow extra cookie sheets, cookie cutters, and bakeware that you only use once a year. Your mother, friends who regularly entertain, or older relatives are good sources for these party supplies. And they will all be glad to have their serving and bakeware used again and for a fun occasion. Who knows, you may even get to keep some of these things if your mom and older relatives don't use them at all anymore.

❊

Keep the food at your party simple, particularly if you're short on money and time. Use recipes for dishes you can make ahead and freeze or refrigerate for several days before the party, like lasagna, baked ziti, casserole-type dishes, soup-mix dips, stuffed breads, etc. This will also prevent that last-minute trip to the grocery store the day of the party.

❊

Have extra trays available for easy pickup of dirty glasses and dishes, so your guests have room for coffee cups and dessert plates. Then you can just place the filled trays on a counter and forget about them until the party ends. (You'll save your rug from dropped glasses and plates of food, too.)

❊

Keep desserts simple, especially if preparing dinner will take up most of your time. Cookies, fudge, and candy all will satisfy your guests just fine. Or consider asking a few of your guests to bring something.

❊

Make easy napkin holders by tying holiday ribbons around the napkins instead of buying elaborate and expensive rings.

And use ribbon to tie napkins and utensils together for the buffet table.

❊

Buy food and nonalcoholic drinks in bulk at discount warehouses or large supermarkets to realize the most savings.

❊

Instead of picking up cold cuts at the deli, cook your own. A boneless ham, roast beef, and turkey breast bought whole from the supermarket are cheaper than what you will pay for the same selection sliced from the deli counter. And your home-baked meats will taste better, too.

Use a deli slicer to cut your meat thin. If you don't have your own, use a friend's or ask at your local deli counter if they will slice it for you for a nominal charge. (If you're a regular customer, they might do it for free.)

Cut up your own fruit and vegetables, too. Instead of buying precut fruit pieces, get whole melons, oranges, pineapples, etc., and slice them yourself with a paring knife or melon baller. Whole carrots, celery, and broccoli are simple to cut up and cheapest when purchased in bulk.

❄

Check out rental and restaurant supply stores for good deals on professional-style serving dishes and cookware.

❄

To control costs, keep your bar tab low by serving a champagne punch or similar drink.

And if you plan to serve wine and liquor, buy only as much as you will need. Guests who do drink alcohol will probably go through two drinks in the first hour and about one each hour after that. So try to plan accordingly when choosing your liquor. Don't buy what no one will drink—skip the Scotch or rye if most of your guests prefer wine or vodka. Why waste the money on something that will sit on a shelf and collect dust for years? If you are unsure of what and how much to buy, check with your local liquor and wine salesperson for some advice. Also ask if you can return any unopened bottles so you're not stuck with the extra.

❄

Go to party-supply stores or discount warehouses to find the best prices on plastic items, like cups, serving dishes, and utensils. These are also good places to find paper products like napkins, plates, and tablecloths.

❄

Just before your guests arrive, turn down the heat so the house doesn't get stuffy an hour or two into the party. Even two or four degrees below the usual setting will keep everyone more comfortable.

## Creative Ideas for Your Party

Sometimes what makes your party successful is a different take on some ordinary things. Like these ideas.

No Christmas party is complete without music. Instead of running a full sampling of Frank or Perry, try mixing your own tapes of favorites from your entire collection. Of course you must have Bing Crosby singing "White Christmas," Elvis Presley's version of "Blue Christmas," and "Rudolph the Red-Nosed

Reindeer" by Gene Autry (yes, the original)! My personal collection includes Steve Lawrence and Eydie Gorme singing "That Holiday Feeling," Burl Ives crooning about "A Holly Jolly Christmas," Emerson, Lake, and Palmer's "Father Christmas," and "Santa Claus Is Comin' to Town" by the Pointer Sisters. And it will be nice to play these same mixes even after the party is over.

Or make different tapes for the various times in your party. For example, you might want only instrumental selections played during dinner, and prefer carols with vocals for after dessert so everyone can sing along. Put together a more upbeat selection that includes songs like "Jingle-Bell Rock" and "Sleigh Ride" to throw on when the party needs a jump start. If you're having a decorating party, put together some songs about trimming the house, like "We Need a Little Christmas" and "Deck the Halls."

To keep the music going all night, assign one of the kids the job of changing the tapes, albums, and/or CDs for the party.

❄

If you and the kids have been making gingerbread people, use them as place cards for your Christmas dinner party. Write each person's name in icing on their gingerbread man or woman and set it at his or her spot at the table. Your guests can take home their place card or eat it for dessert!

❄

Bring the true spirit of the holidays to your party by asking everyone to bring a present or toy to be donated to a charity that hands out gifts to poor children and families. You can mention the organization in your invitation and even offer gift ideas.

❉

Set up a coffee bar for dessert, away from the buffet table, using specialty coffees and liqueurs. This will keep guests out of the kitchen and allow you to put cleanup off until later, after everyone has left. It's also a great way to stimulate conversation among your guests.

## Making Your Event a Hit

So many things make a party successful, but the mix of guests can make or break your event. This is especially true if you invite people from all parts of your life—work, neighborhood, family, church, school, etc. You want everyone to socialize and get to know each other, but that's not always the case. Sometimes you have to work at getting things going and keeping them rolling. Here are some ideas on how to do that.

The larger your party, the larger the mix of people. With so many folks milling around, no one will really notice who's talking with whom. But when it's a small affair, all of the people should know each other relatively well; otherwise, you'll find a few wallflowers hiding out.

❄

Set food out in each of the rooms where you want your guests to mingle. Otherwise, people will congregate only in the kitchen and dining room, the usual hangouts. Place different foods in different rooms to motivate everyone to walk around and chat with the other guests. This also keeps your kitchen clear as a work area for you and your helpers.

❄

Include at least one couple on your "to invite" list who you know socializes well with just about everyone. This way you're not the only one working the room, and you know someone is out there breaking the ice.

❄

If you plan to let your kids attend the party, invite friends with children the same age as yours to keep the younger crowd amused. Even the most well-behaved kids get bored and whiny when there's no one around to play with but adults.

❄

Games are a great way to get people to mix. Pull out Trivial Pursuit, Scattergories, Pictionary, Charades, etc. If possible, try to take a holiday twist with whatever you decide to play.

❄

Your guests will take their cue from you. So get out there and mix. Besides, what kind of party will it be if the host doesn't spend time with each guest?

❄

Introduce your guests to each other. Think ahead of time what some of them might have in common—a fondness for computers, a favorite vacation spot, an alma mater, a football team. Sometimes people just need someone else to get the conversation started for them.

❄

Make sure *you* are having a good time. Because if you're bored with the party and the guests, well, everyone else will be, too. And the opposite holds true as well: if you are at ease, your guests will be, too. That means not freaking out when someone spills the red punch all over your carpet, or running around from room to room making sure everyone has enough to eat but not staying long enough to chat with anyone. Parties are fun, so enjoy yours. RELAX!

# ❄❄❄❄❄❄❄❄❄❄ 4

# *Gift-Giving Made Easy*

In recent years the whole idea of giving gifts at Christmas has gotten out of hand. Instead of being one small part of Christmas, it has become the main focus of an overly commercialized holiday. Too many of us wind up debt-ridden by the end of the season. Not exactly the true meaning of Christmas, is it? So it's time to rethink gift-giving—and make it fun for everyone again.

Because the truly meaningful gifts, the ones that people are most grateful to receive and that make you realize what Christmas is all about, require some thought but not necessarily a lot of money. This chapter offers plenty of ideas for even the most hard-to-buy-for person on your list. You can create gifts with your own hands and give presents that come straight from the heart. Read on to find out what you can give this year. Because picking and giving gifts should be fun, not a chore!

## Sharing the Spirit of the Season

When you care a lot about Christmas, you want everyone else to share your excitement for the holiday. These gifts do just that.

If you consider yourselves a musical family, make your own Christmas tape. Everyone can pull out his or her instrument of choice (the kids might even have some Christmas music they've been practicing with their guitar/piano/clarinet teacher), or you can go it a cappella. Practice for a few nights before you tape so that everyone can learn the right words to the songs (most of us have our own variation on even the most popular Christmas carols), and you can try to create some nice harmony, too. Then hook up the microphones and start recording. Your tape will probably end up filled with plenty of giggles and talking in between all the singing. Leave all of it in because it will make the grandparents, and anyone else who will be listening, love your tape even more.

❄

Practically all of us have at least one older relative who has decided putting up a full-size Christmas tree and most of their other decorations is more than they can handle this year. But you know they missed the smell of the pine and having some symbol of the holiday in their house. So buy a miniature Christmas tree from a discount store, five-and-dime, local nursery, or even the hardware store. You can buy one already decorated, too. Since these potted trees are live, offer to plant it for them in the spring as part of your gift.

❋

In the true spirit of the holiday, take the money you planned to spend on material presents and donate it to various charities (whether they're medical, environmental, or humanitarian) in the names of the folks on your Christmas list. Then write out cards for everyone telling them what you did—how much you gave, to whom, and even why you chose the particular organization.

❋

I love reading aloud with my children, and Christmas stories are no exception. Even toddlers who aren't old enough to read can often "read" a story practically word for word that they have heard many times. So make an audiotape of some of your family's favorites for the grandparents, special friends, or anyone else you know would love it. Parents of small children might be especially appreciative. Some of the best books include: *How the Grinch Stole Christmas!* by Dr. Seuss, *The Night Before Christmas* by Clement C. Moore, *The Littlest Angel* by Charles Tazewell, *The Tree that Came to Stay* by Anna Quindlen, *A Christmas Carol* by Charles Dickens, and, of course, the original Christmas story as it appears in the Bible, Luke: Chapters 1 and 2, Matthew: Chapters 1 and 2.

## Gift-Giving Made Easy

✱

Instead of buying material gifts for your immediate family, have everyone chip in what they would have spent on each other and, as a family, donate the money to an agreed-upon charity. Or, if you still want to give each other a few smaller presents, take some of the money planned for gift buying and give it to a favorite cause.

✱

Arrange a plate filled with all the delights of your Christmas dinner to bring to a neighbor down the street who isn't able to get out for the holiday. Have a few family members come along for the visit, too. And don't forget to include some dessert!

✱

Contact a local church or the Salvation Army to find a family you can help through the holidays with extra food, clothing, or gifts. Or ask about sponsoring a family for a year. You can make this an annual tradition and help a different family beginning each Christmas. This could be one gift your family gives itself each year.

### With Your Own Two Hands

You don't have to be a certified craftsperson to make attractive gifts. Here are a few simple things you can do alone or with your kids.

You can make this easy gumdrop tree yourself for anyone with a taste for candy on your list. But the kids will love making, as well as eating, this one, and they can bring it to school as a class present.

WHAT YOU'LL NEED: A 12-inch-high foam tree stand and a box of toothpicks; a bag of miniature, multicolored gumdrops.

WHAT TO DO: Stick toothpicks all over the tree from top to bottom. Then place gumdrops on the end of each "branch," pushing them in only as far as necessary to be secure—you don't want any points exposed ready to stick anyone. Place a cluster of gumdrops on one to three toothpicks as a treetop.

VARIATIONS: You can use all green gumdrops on the branches to make it look more like a real Christmas tree and top off with a single red drop.

❄

Ornaments are always a good gift, especially for young children. A friend made this unbreakable ornament from a wooden letter block for our daughter.

WHAT YOU'LL NEED: One wooden letter block from your preschooler's set with the first letter of the name of the person you will be giving the ornament to; glitter glue in whatever color(s) you like; a black fine-point marker; a six- to eight-inch piece of cord to use as a hanger; glue; very small holiday figurine for the top (optional).

## Gift-Giving Made Easy

WHAT TO DO: Outline the borders, pictures, and other letters on the block with the black marker. Then cover the featured letter with glitter glue. Let dry. Glue the cord to the bottom of the ornament making sure the block is centered. When it dries, tie a tight bow with the two loose ends to create the hanger. Glue a small holiday bear or mouse or other mini-decoration to the top of the block (optional).

VARIATIONS: You can outline the letter in one color and fill it in with another. Or you can outline the other letters and pictures on the block with glitter glue or colored marker instead of the black fine point.

❄

Your favorite gardener can always use an extra pair of work gloves. Here's how to personalize the set you give.

WHAT YOU'LL NEED: A pair of cloth gardening gloves; acrylic paint.

WHAT TO DO: Paint the person's initials, name, favorite flower, or vegetable on the top of each glove. Let dry and your gift is done.

❄

For bird lovers or bird-watchers on your list, make a bird feeder.

WHAT YOU'LL NEED: A pinecone; peanut butter; dinner knife; a bowl at least slightly larger than the pinecone; loose birdseed; strong string, such as dental floss.

WHAT TO DO: Coat the pinecone completely with peanut butter. Pour the birdseed in a bowl. Roll the coated pinecone in the birdseed and cover it all. Then tie a piece of string to the top of the pinecone to use as the hanger (make sure the piece is long enough to fit around a branch and still hang down).

VARIATIONS: Instead of a pinecone, use a piece of stale (but not completely hard) bread cut into holiday shapes (cookie cutters can make this job easy). Spread peanut butter on one or both sides of the bread, then pour birdseed over the coated side. Make a small hole at the top and thread a string through it as a hanger.

## From Your House to Theirs

There are lots of things sitting, standing, and hiding in your house that can be turned into presents, or used to create some. Check out these ideas.

Do you often pass your overcrowded bookshelves and tell yourself that you really have to do something with all of those books that you love so much, but will never read again? Instead of leaving the clutter and letting the books go unused, pass them on to some special people on your list this Christmas. Betty Crocker and Fanny Farmer cookbooks that you haven't opened in years are good for those folks just starting out on their own and who might need some cooking lessons. That collection of best-loved children's bedtime stories can go to the newest baby in the family. And a book you treasured back in high school might be appreciated by your favorite teenager. Check around on your shelves and see what else you can give away. Then, to personalize the gift, write a short note inside the front cover explaining whose bookshelf the book came from and why you are passing it on.

❋

If baking your own gingerbread house seems impossible this year, then buy one already baked, but that you (and the kids) construct and decorate. Still cheaper than the pre-baked-and-built variety, it will require a lot less of your time than one you make completely from scratch. And it's best for the children who are too young to work near hot stoves and mixers, and who have too little patience to wait for the baking and cooling. You can probably get it all put together on a rainy or snowy day in December. Then bring this as the gift to whomever you share Christmas dinner with this year.

❋

My spider plant sometimes goes wild reproducing itself, but I hate to cut off and throw away all those baby plants. If you have the same problem, pick up a pretty flowerpot and some potting soil and place one or two cuttings (that have been rooted in water) from any of your plants in the potted soil. You can even include a small piece of paper with special instructions on how to care for the plant, especially if the recipient is known for having a brown thumb. Then tie a pretty ribbon around the flowerpot, and there you go.

❉

Does anyone on your list have a fireplace? Save scraps of wood from fallen branches, wood craft sets, etc., and some old newspapers and put them in a decorative container, like a small brass pot, for kindling that can go next to the fireplace.

Or if you have a tree removed from your property, chop and tie it up for anyone with a wood-burning stove or fireplace. They won't mind the free delivery, either.

❉

Any survivors from your summer garden, like winter squash or herbs that you have dried, make good gifts. Place the herbs in empty spice jars and relabel. The vegetables will look nice placed in a basket lined with a patterned kitchen towel.

❉

Has someone mentioned how much they love your soup tureen or strawberry pot? If there are special items around your house that are in very good condition but you no longer use, wrap them up. Then add a little note explaining that this present is coming from your home to theirs in hopes that they will use it often and think of you when they do.

※

Share your favorite or most popular recipes by creating your own cookbook or recipe box. Write out the ingredients and directions for making your vegetable lasagna, chicken chow mein, cranberry sauce, apple cake, stuffed mushrooms, date-and-nut bread, etc., on white or color-coded index cards. Put the cards in wooden boxes or photo albums and give to all the bakers on your list, or anyone who could use some new cooking ideas. If you have a lot of recipes, make your own book. Type everything out on full-size sheets of paper, then get it copied and bound at your local printer. You can even include an opening page that explains who the recipe book came from and why.

※

Give seeds from your summer fruits, vegetables, and flowers as gifts so other people can start their own gardens. Place the seeds in small glass jars, plastic containers, or cardboard boxes and label them. Don't forget to include a set of instructions for when, where, and how to plant the seeds. This might be a good idea for some of the kids on your list, too.

## Yummy Treats

Pop open those cabinets and pull out your recipe cards. A bunch of gift ideas are sitting in your kitchen just waiting to be discovered. Here are a few you might want to try.

Do you have a favorite cookie, bread, soup, or dip recipe that lots of people have been asking for or trying to copy unsuccessfully? Give them the recipe and ingredients all dressed up in a decorative container.

Fill an inexpensive glass jar or clear plastic container with the dry ingredients. For example, if you plan on sharing your vegetarian chili recipe, alternate layers of each of the three types of dried beans. Then put a piece of plastic wrap on top of that and add all of your spices, like the chili powder, salt, and cayenne pepper. Write out the recipe on an index card. Fold it in half, poke a hole in the top corner, and string some yarn or colored cord through the hole to tie the card to the jar. Put the lid on and your gift is ready to go.

❆

Instead of making your basic three-dozen recipe of sugar cookies, make six dozen. Multiply the other batches of cookies you were going to make, too, and give the extras as gifts. Put the cookies in holiday tins you either collected over the years or can buy cheap.

❆

Rather than buying chocolate to give as gifts, make your own. You'll be surprised how easy it is. Stop in at your local chocolate shop or department store for all the ingredients (and easy directions) to do it yourself. Set aside a Saturday for this family project. The kids can make chocolate lollipops for their friends, and you can make a variety of flavors and designs that can be packaged simply in a holiday tin or clear container, then decorated with a bow. This is a great gift for the entire office—bring in a container for everyone to share. Relatives and friends will enjoy every mouthwatering bite.

❊

You and the kids usually spend hours baking and decorating gingerbread men, and after the first dozen or so, you all get a little bored painting on the same faces and outfits. This year use your whole array of Christmas cookie cutters to make holiday shapes out of gingerbread. (We even use our nonholiday varieties, including our now-famous alligator shape, too. The green icing makes him dressed for the holiday.) You'll all like the change, and everyone you give them to will still enjoy eating one of the best flavors of Christmas. Try making a Christmas tree complete with multicolored ornaments, a stocking outlined in red, a striped candy cane, even Rudolph and his red nose.

❊

If you like taking the time to make your own pasta or jelly, or canning your own pickles, set aside jars for gifts this year. With only a little extra time and a few dollars, you can make gifts that take a lot less time than shopping. And most of your gifts can be prepared weeks and possibly even months before Christmas.

❄

If everyone you know will be baking cookies this year, bake bread instead. Use up ripened bananas, leftover bags of fresh cranberries you didn't need for Thanksgiving, that spare box of raisins, or the extra cans of pumpkin that you forgot you had. These are the key ingredients in some simple quick-bread recipes. Make a large batch and wrap the loaves in plastic wrap and foil, then tie on a pretty bow. You can always bake the bread ahead of time and freeze the loaves until you're ready to give them away.

❄

Who doesn't love fudge? Find your favorite recipe (or the simplest one, if you're really busy) and fill holiday containers for anyone on your list.

❄

You like the idea of a food basket, but the usual summer-sausage-and-cheese variety doesn't inspire you. Pick up your favorite ingredients and a basket and make your own.

## Gift-Giving Made Easy 71

For friends who are watching their weight or following special diets, put together sugar-free/fat-free/wheat-free muffins, all-fruit spreads, low-sugar jams, pure maple or all-fruit syrup, fresh or canned fruit, and shelled nuts and seeds. You can make a breakfast basket with syrup, jam, fruit butters, sample-size containers of tea and coffee, muffins, and pancake/waffle mix.

Get a snack basket together with dried fruit, cookies, and nuts; or one filled with the makings for ice-cream sundaes—sprinkles, chocolate and butterscotch syrup, cookies and candies to be crumbled, even an ice-cream scoop.

You can make your own variation on the traditional fruit basket by including some tropical favorites like pineapple, kiwi, and papaya, if you can find them in your area. Just be sure not to buy too early or the fruit will be overripe by the time you deliver the basket.

❋

For the people on your list who like confections, pick out some pretty glass jars and bulk bags of candy. Fill the jars with various sweets for an attractive, delicious, and inexpensive gift for some of your candy lovers. Place a bow on top or tie a ribbon around the middle. This makes a perfect gift for your weekend baby-sitter, the kids' school or music teachers, and even the neighbors. They'll be especially flattered if you remember what their favorite types of candy are and go out of your way to include them.

## Remember This

Hold on to the important moments in life by passing on reminders of special times with the people you care about most.

Go through your boxes of extra pictures of your kids, of yourselves, and even of your friends. Then fill a collage photo frame or a photo album with all the pictures and give to grandparents, parents, old friends, or even your children. Include shots of you and your best friend as kids, in each other's wedding, on a favorite vacation. I gave my parents a framed photo collage of my older sister and me that included my sister in her first car, the two of us on our favorite family vacation, me in my playpen, and my sister at a high school dance club practice. Put together your own collage and give someone a truly priceless gift.

❄

Head to the newsstand on the day your best friend gets married, your niece or nephew is born, or the day your son or daughter graduates college for a copy of your favorite newspaper. Save it until Christmas and give as a gift to whomever's special day it was. Who wouldn't want to look back at what happened in the world on the day they were born, married, or even promoted?

❄

Take a printed invitation from a wedding, anniversary party, christening, or graduation and frame it for whomever's event it was. You can even frame a saying or poem that has special meaning for someone on your list.

## Practical, Yet Truly Appreciated

Shopping for Christmas gifts gets very frustrating when you pick out presents not knowing whether any of the people you are buying for will even like them. Here are sure hits for many of the people on your list.

How many times have you walked into your parents' house and noticed a worn-out bedspread, hall rug, or pair of curtains that your folks just will not replace because they consider it too expensive? If you can afford it, this Christmas take it upon yourself to buy a new toaster, lace tablecloth, set of towels, etc. If you wonder about picking the correct style, get a gift certificate to the store where they can purchase it, or write a note that says you will take them shopping to get the particular present after the holidays.

❄

The problem with many expensive gifts is that they end up being used only at special times, like a piece of crystal, or a china serving platter. Though we all like to receive the fancy items we cannot afford to buy for ourselves, it can be better to give things that can be used regularly—silverware, an inexpensive camera, even a small table lamp. Look around at some of the things you use all the time—someone else might find them useful, too.

✻

This year buy a copy of that John Wayne movie your dad's always talking about or that Cary Grant film your mom loves so much but can never seem to find on television anymore. You can get lots of films on tape for under $20, including some for less than $10. And three-tape sets are even cheaper than buying videos individually. If you think your parents (or whoever) would prefer to pick out their own, get them a membership or gift certificate to the local video rental store.

✻

Candles are always appreciated, particularly by people who entertain often (or, on a more practical level, those who live in areas that have frequent blackouts). Though inexpensive, candles really add a touch of luxury. They're perfect for a friend who likes to unwind with a warm, quiet bath by candlelight or for a couple who enjoy romantic dinners at home. Card stores, craft shows, and department stores all carry wide selections to choose from.

✻

Have a friend who likes to grow their own every summer? Give a starter kit—seeds, potting soil, and

## Gift-Giving Made Easy 77

containers to start plants indoors. You can order all you need through catalogs or find everything at a hardware store where you can get information on exactly what to buy.

An indoor herb garden kit can work for an apartment dweller who likes to cook with fresh seasonings, but has no place to plant outdoors. Some kits come in sizes that fit perfectly in most windowsills.

❄

Families, new car owners, weekend athletes, parents with kids on sports teams—they can all use a first-aid or car emergency kit. You can buy them already made, or put one together yourself.

For a first-aid kit you will want to include bandages of various sizes, an antibiotic cream, hydrogen peroxide, gauze wrap, tape, an Ace bandage, and an ice pack that doesn't require refrigeration.

In a car emergency kit you will need a blanket, flashlight with batteries, window scraper, nonperishable food like nuts and bottled water, booster cables, warning triangles, fire extinguisher, and some basic tools like a hammer, screwdriver (both a flathead and a Phillips), and wrench.

❄

We all have trouble remembering important dates, like birthdays and anniversaries. For those on your list who have an especially hard time, buy a calendar and fill in all the special events of the coming year. You can even decorate it with pictures of each person on their day, and stickers that say "Happy Birthday" or "Remember This."

※

Track sales at the local five-and-dime for sewing supplies for that someone on your list who still knows how to use a needle and thread. Refills of notions, borders, thread, needles, even thimbles can make a useful gift, especially if they arrive in a new sewing basket or box.

## Heartfelt Gifts

Some of the most meaningful Christmas gifts are not found in the mall.

What is the one thing that all parents crave? A night alone without the kids. So instead of *buying* your best friends a gift, give them a certificate for your baby-sitting services—they do whatever they like while you watch their kids. Or you can give them an invitation to dinner at your house without the children, and you take care of the baby-sitter's bill. This inexpensive gift will mean a lot more than anything you could have found for them in a store.

※

Commit yourself to handling the lawn-mowing, leaf-blowing, and/or snow-shoveling duties in the new year for an elderly relative or neighbor who can no longer care for their property by themselves or who cannot afford to hire someone to do the work for them.

✻

Give a friend or relative a gift certificate to a day with you at your favorite museum, botanical garden, or zoo. This way you can spend time together and also visit a place you never seem to go to as often as you would like. You can even use this as a gift to friends with kids, and all of you can share a day doing something a little different and a bit cultural. Include brochures from the various places to help everyone decide where to go.

✻

You know your friends like to get away for the weekend once in a while, or that your parents want to go visit their other grandchildren out of town, but they hate leaving the house empty or putting the dog in the kennel. Promise to take care of the dog-watching or house-sitting services as your gift this year.

✻

If your kids complain that you never seem to spend enough time with them, doing what they want to do (what child doesn't?), then stuff their stockings with certificates for a trip to the movies, a lunch date, or a shopping trip with Mom and/or Dad.

If you don't have kids of your own, but like spending time with your nieces, nephews, or friends' kids, give them certificates for a sleepover at your place or a fun-filled day with you.

❄

Invite the friends you normally exchange gifts with for an adults-only formal dinner at your house as your present to them this year. You can request that everyone dress for the occasion, and even include the menu if you know what you would like to serve.

❄

Take elderly or homebound friends or relatives shopping for the holidays as your gift. Or offer to do it after the new year, when fewer people are likely to make the gesture, but when your friend will probably need it most.

## For the Kids

Deciding on presents for the members of the junior set on your list is challenging, whether or not you have kids of your own. And considering that they will be getting plenty from Santa Claus, you don't want to give repeats or outdo the big guy. Here are some ideas that should cover it.

If you decide to go the toy route, you can "play it safe," yet be a surefire hit by adding on to a favorite toy set the kids already own, like another box of Lego blocks, a new car for the wooden train set, extra cups and saucers for a tea set, more modeling clay. These are things most other people will not pick out. And parents never object if their children can get more use out of an old toy.

❊

Pass on your childhood toys that are still in good shape to kids who are a little older and can appreciate them. These can include a Raggedy Ann, Tonka trucks, Lionel trains. Toys that are no longer available are especially impressive.

❊

Young children, those three to eight, will love old-fashioned cookie cutters that can be used to make cookies, cutouts with Play-Doh, as stencils, and even to cut sandwiches. The plastic variety are best because they have no sharp edges.

❊

Feeling guilty about tossing out all that junk mail you get at work and at home? If the paper comes with writing on just one side, use a three-hole punch and make a binder of drawing paper for preschoolers who cannot read the words on the back. A box of crayons or a set of watercolors will finish it off.

Or if there are pictures in the junk mail, paste various shots on the blank side of the paper for an ABC book for those same kids.

❊

Gifts that contribute to a child's education are appreciated by almost every parent. Savings bonds are still a good bet, especially for preschoolers, because the bonds will reach maturity while they are going to college. But you can buy stock or transfer some of your own shares for older children. Talk with your broker about how to set this up.

Or open a savings account with a bank that has special savings plans for kids or programs that teach children about spending and saving money.

❄

Some of my young children's most treasured gifts are ones they received from craft shows. Our best friend has picked up a handmade rag doll, miniature carousel, hand puppet, and early-American spinning top at these fairs for our kids. You can find reasonable prices and original toys here, too.

### For Your Coworkers

Who doesn't agonize over who to buy for—and what to buy—at the job. Okay, so the boss knows she has to get a gift for everyone, but no one else is ever really sure. And sometimes it's just so hard to find the money to cover all the people you think you should. Don't worry, here are some great ideas that will take care of it for you.

Send around a memo to everyone in your work group (mainly the people you would expect to exchange gifts with) that suggests all of you chip in money and make a donation to a favorite charity instead of giving presents to each other. Set a date to select the organization and determine how much everyone should put in. One person can be in charge of collecting and sending the money.

❇

Sometimes gifts feel like a waste because they're too small to really send any kind of message. What will share your holiday sentiments more effectively is having the whole group go out to lunch or dinner (everyone pays their own way) and spend some time together away from the job. And around holiday time, everyone can use a few hours relaxing over a nice meal with friends.

❇

Picking out a present for each person you work with is difficult. But you can avoid that by giving a gift to the group as a whole. Bake a large batch of cookies and put them out where everyone has access to them. Include a little note that says who baked them and why you made them. Or, instead of cookies, throw everyone's favorite candies into a large container, bake a cake, bring in doughnuts or bagels, or even buy a coffeemaker if your area doesn't have one.

❇

Kris Kringle (also known as Secret Santa) works well in large or small groups. Everyone's name is put into a bag and each person pulls out one name. This name belongs to the only coworker they will be buying for this year. As a group, determine how much everyone should spend. Part of the fun is leaving small gifts around for each other in the weeks before Christmas, but you can also decide to save a slightly more expensive present for the last day when you all find out who your Kris Kringles are. This type of giving also guarantees that everyone in the group will receive a present this year.

❋

If the company is not throwing a Christmas party, have everyone chip in for one instead of exchanging presents. A few people can be in charge of finding a place, setting a date and time, and deciding what will be served. It doesn't have to be an elaborate event, just a chance for everyone to get together and feel as if you are all celebrating the holiday together.

If a big party will take too much planning, or more money than most people would like to spend, keep it simple and in the work area. Everyone can bring some type of food or drink. Make a list of what should be at the party and have each person sign up for something. The last day on the job before the holiday is probably the best day to celebrate, since people are rarely motivated to get much work done on Christmas Eve.

❋

Forget about buying gifts for the adults. If everyone in your group has kids, then decide that you will all pick up something small for each other's children. You might want to have your own kids help you decide what to buy. It wouldn't hurt for everyone to settle on a price range for the presents, either.

❋

Have a kitchen at your office or shop? Then arrange for a group breakfast. Maybe the bosses can do the cooking, and everyone else can bring things like plates, napkins, eating utensils, syrup, etc.

If there is no cooking area, then bring in bagels, doughnuts, muffins, croissants, Danish, and pastry instead. A few bottles of juice and some coffee and you're all set.

## To Satisfy the Hard-to-Buy-For

Someone on your list always gets put off to the last minute as you struggle to think of a gift idea . . . *any* gift idea. But even that impossible person can use something. Check out these suggestions.

If every year you have the hardest time trying to decide what to get for your siblings and their spouses and kids, and complain about what all these gifts are doing to your budget, then do a "grab bag" with your family this year. Each person buys only one thing and for only one person.

Sometime in November when you are all together (not later than Thanksgiving weekend) put everyone's name in a bag and let each person pick (no one should be buying for someone in their immediate family). This becomes the only person in the family they will buy a present for this year. Then set a price range for the gift, which should be more than you usually spend on any one person, but much less than the total cost of what you would have bought for everyone in the family.

If there are young children in the family, aunts and uncles and grandparents may still want to buy for them. That's fine, as long as everyone agrees on it.

❊

Instead of one gift for the year, share one every month. Magazine subscriptions are a great idea for anyone who likes to read, and plenty can be bought for under $20. If you're a subscriber yourself, you might find even better deals on gift subscriptions. With so many specialty publications available, you can find one for the kids, your in-laws, even your grandparents. You can renew their subscriptions every Christmas, or try a different magazine each year.

Begin checking magazines in October for gift subscription forms. Many publications will send a card to your gift recipient that says you bought the subscription and when the first issue should arrive. This will cover those out-of-town gifts you usually send too late.

❊

## Gift-Giving Made Easy 87

Many nonprofit and charitable organizations sell gifts through mail-order catalogs or shops. Usually a percentage of each purchase goes directly to the particular charity, and the gifts include information on the organization and how the sale of this gift helped the cause. Many of the items they sell are unique and carry some significance for the organization.

These are just a few of the charities that have their own mail-order catalogs or flyers with gifts and cards available for the Christmas holidays. Check with the local chapter of your favorite charitable organization to find out if they have something similar available.

National Wildlife Federation: 1-800-432-6564
UNICEF (United Nations Children's Fund): 1-800-553-1200
Amnesty International: 212-807-8400
Habitat for Humanity International: 1-800-422-4828 ext. 312

Trying to find a gift for each person in a family of four can be impossible. So this time around find something they can all use together, like sports equipment, a pair of headphones for the stereo, an ice-cream maker, a newspaper subscription, even a waffle iron. The present is likely to cost less than the total cost of four individual gifts, and will be appreciated and used more.

❆

Books are gifts that work for everyone on your list. What better way to let your best friend know you value her quiet time than to give her a way to relax and tune out the stresses of the day? By giving books to kids, you create an environment for them to spend time with their parents and siblings reading aloud. And books help fill days for people who are homebound for any period of time. Check out books on tape for anyone who spends hours on the road, or has a hard time reading small print.

You can do practically all your shopping in bookstores, so spend lots of time in one or two, looking closely for the right book for each person on your list, because you will not be running through the other 150 stores in the mall this year.

❅

Help folks decorate their Christmas tree by giving ornaments—something more detailed than your basic glass ball. Craft shows are filled with unique creations for the tree and are a great place to find personalized ornaments, too. But department stores, card shops, and specialty stores all have a selection of balls and figurines, and at least one to please each person on your list.

We have received many ornaments as gifts over the years (and given out just as many) and enjoy remembering who gave them to us as we put up the tree each year.

❅

If you just cannot find the right gift, or know that you could never figure out what a fussy teenager on

## Gift-Giving Made Easy

your list would really like, purchase a gift certificate at a store where you are sure they shop. The opportunity to go into a favorite store with "free money" is a winner with almost everyone. Don't worry about whether the amount is enough or that a certificate can seem impersonal. You could spend more on something they will hate and never use, and what does that really have to do with Christmas?

❄❄❄❄❄❄❄❄❄❄ 5

# All the Trimmings

It seems so simple. You head into your favorite department store to pick up a few new Christmas decorations, a box or two of cards, and some wrapping paper. But even before you get to the checkout, you know that you're going over your budget again. And the excitement you had when you walked into the store begins to wane.

But it doesn't have to be this way. The makings for the best trimmings already live in your house, or require only a few inexpensive items from a discount store or craft shop. Read through this chapter for ideas on decorating your house and tree, as well as making your own Christmas cards and gift wraps. All the handmade trimmings require minimal artistic skill and only a little bit of time. The kids can join in on most of these, too. And what better way to celebrate Christmas than with decorations the whole family had a hand in?

## Getting Creative with What's Around the House

It's hard to believe that some of your nicest Christmas trimmings are within arm's reach, but it's true.

That spare bag of fresh cranberries sitting in your refrigerator since Thanksgiving can be strung with popcorn and wrapped around your tree in place of tinsel garland. Pop your own popcorn (or buy a big bag of prepopped at the supermarket) and, using a needle and a long piece of thread (or dental floss), string the popcorn and cranberries intermittently. Create patterns or go for a whatever-I-feel-like design. You can make one long strand, or string several, varying the pattern of each. If the kids wear thimbles, they can help, too—just be sure they don't eat all the popcorn.

❊

Instead of buying ornament hangers, use paper clips to hold the decorations on the tree. Use paper clips to hold unfilled stockings, too.

❊

I used to watch friends create easy Christmas decorations by studding oranges with whole cloves. I liked the scent and how they looked, but never knew what to call them—until now. Pomanders.

All you need are oranges and/or lemons, whole cloves, and some ribbon (optional). Stud the orange or lemon with the cloves (if the cloves break when you try to pierce the skin, use a toothpick or bamboo skewer to make the initial puncture). You can cover the fruit completely with the cloves, or create a pattern and leave room to tie a ribbon around the middle.

Set the pomanders in bowls or other open containers around the house. Mix them with pinecones found in your yard for an attractive centerpiece.

❇

Why buy a tree skirt when you can make one yourself with a spare white bedsheet? Wrap the sheet loosely around the base of the tree and over the stand to look like snow. If your tree is fresh, leave an opening in the back for watering.

❇

Fill glass jars with holiday candies and place around your house as decorations and easy-access snacks.

❇

For a safe way to decorate the bedrooms of school-age kids, try this:

Pick through a bucket of wooden letter blocks to spell out the words *MERRY CHRISTMAS* in all capitals. With a red glitter pen, cover the letters and borders of the blocks for the word *MERRY*. With a green glitter pen, cover the letters and borders of the blocks for the word *CHRISTMAS*. (Or make variations on this color combination, like alternating the red and green with each letter.) When all the glitter has dried, line up the blocks in order and place on a child's dresser or bookshelf, or even on your fireplace mantel or dinner table. Bonus: If they get knocked over, they won't break!

❄

Hollow out red apples to use as candleholders. You can use votive candles or tapers, depending upon how wide you make the holes. Once the candles are in place, set the holders on small, heat-safe dishes or trays to protect tables from melted wax.

When the season is over, cut up the apples and throw the pieces out for the squirrels and birds.

❄

String holiday ribbons through thick Bavarian-style pretzels to create a chain link that can be hung across a mantle, down a stairway, or above a doorway.

❄

When decorating for the holidays, what most of us want is at least one room in our house to make us, and our guests, feel the spirit of Christmas as soon as we enter it. To do that, you need to give each room a focal point that highlights the theme of that part of the house or apartment. My parents use their living room fireplace, including the mantel and wall above it, to share their feelings about the holiday. They set the manger in the center of the mantel and surround it on both sides with ceramic angels holding candles and old, painted cardboard houses. The edge of the mantel gets trimmed with white lights wrapped around green garland. A second set of white lights runs across the back to illuminate both the houses and the manger.

On the mirrored wall above this is an artificial wreath that my mother decorates herself each Christmas with plastic apples, berries, pinecones, and holly. And just below the mantel hang our stockings, with all of our names on them. Complementing the mantel, and finishing off the room, is the live Christmas tree which stands only a few feet away in the back corner, decorated with white lights and tinsel and lots of ornaments.

You can try something similar in the rooms of your home. Or concentrate on decorating just one room, possibly combining several themes, like my mother does. That might mean bringing the manger out from under the tree so it can easily be seen, or putting a fresh wreath inside the house as well as outside this year.

※

Take small gold or colored Christmas balls and place them in clear glass goblets. Set on end tables, mantels, and dining tables as decorations.

Or fill a large crystal bowl, pitcher, or ice bucket with the larger colored balls for a glistening centerpiece.

## All the Trimmings

❄

Instead of buying Christmas candlesticks, tie holiday ribbons around the base of a pair you already own.

❄

Decorate your mailbox this year by attaching pieces of ribbon with clear, all-weather tape in a striped design. You can feel like you are opening a present each time you reach in to pull out your latest batch of Christmas cards.

❄

Fill a wicker basket with Christmas books of different sizes and for all ages. Then you and the kids can read aloud and get in the spirit of the season any time. And the basket adds a warm touch to any room.

❄

Tie red or green ribbons at the top of cookie cutters and hang them in your windows. Or attach them to the bottom of shades as decoration for the pull strings.

❄

Fill a basket with apples and pinecones, and tie a ribbon on the handle or at one end for a simple centerpiece.

Place candy canes on the tree as ornaments, but skip the wire hangers for these.

❄

Make a festive cookie tray by draping a cake stand with a piece of holiday fabric. Place your cookies on top and there you go.

❄

Take an attractive plain mirror (one without a handle) and put a dozen or so white, red, and/or green votive candles in glass holders on top of it. Place on a dining or coffee table as a centerpiece.

❄

Tie bundles of cinnamon sticks with holiday ribbons and tuck them into a wreath.

❄

Decorate a mantel or coffee table by interspersing candles (in glass containers or on small heat-safe plates) with Christmas cards and clear bowls of potpourri. (Never leave lit candles unattended.)

❄

Place popcorn, pinecones, and greens in a bowl with various-sized candles for a simple centerpiece.

❆

Decorate outdoor trees for birds and squirrels. String popcorn-and-cranberry garlands around evergreens. Or coat pinecones with peanut butter, roll in bird seed, and hang on trees to feed your feathered friends.

Cut stale, but not hard, bread into Christmas shapes and hang as food ornaments for the birds.

Or make small bird feeders with oranges. Cut an orange in half and remove the pulp (use it in a fruit salad or eat it plain) so you have an empty shell. Put holes on both sides of the shell and thread strong string through as a hanger, tying or knotting the ends. Fill the gutted halves with birdseed or suet and hang on trees. Repeat with as many oranges as you like.

❆

Arrange your holiday CDs or cassette boxes on a shelf with the covers showing so they are both decorative and functional.

## Make Your Own Christmas Cards

You can avoid searching through the hundreds of different greetings with these ideas for making them yourself.

We no longer buy and mail Christmas cards to most of our friends and relatives. Instead we write a newsletter sharing our events of the year, updating folks on the goings on of our friends and family in various parts of the country, and extending our good wishes for the holiday. Not only does this save us a lot of money on store-bought cards, it saves the time involved in writing personal notes to the almost 100 people on our list. Our newsletters have become so popular that friends and relatives write us notes in their Christmas cards, telling of their anticipation for this year's installment.

If this idea works for you, pick up paper and envelopes in bulk at a discount office supply store. Type an original on your computer or typewriter. Each family member can write their own section filled with all their news. Then everyone can help fill in the latest on friends and relatives (if you want to include that news, too). Put someone in charge of checking for spelling errors, accuracy, and clarity (you want to avoid confusing your readers).

Next, photocopy your newsletter—check your list ahead of time so you only make as many copies as you will be sending (we usually make a few extra in case we forget anyone). The kids can draw, stamp, or paste decorations on each page to add a touch of Christmas.

Set aside one night for everyone to fold the letters and address, stamp, and stuff the envelopes. Mail the batch the next day and you're done.

❄

## All the Trimmings

You can make your own Christmas cards with blank cards—available in many art-supply stores—or plain postcards. Use a holiday rubber stamp and red or green stamp pad to create your own design. No two cards need be decorated the same.

Then write your original message inside. If you want to use the same message in each card, order a rubber stamp with the imprint from an office supply or novelty store. Then sign the cards and mail. (Remember that postcards use cheaper stamps, too.)

❄

Help the kids make their own Christmas cards to give to their friends and grandparents. Fold pieces of red or green construction paper in half width-wise. Let the kids place stickers and/or stamp a design on the front cover. Inside they can decorate more or write a message and sign it. Cards like these are best hand-delivered and need no envelopes.

❄

If you have a home computer, check in your local computer store for software, paper, and envelopes to make your own Christmas cards on your Mac or PC. With the right program, you can take care of printing everything, including the return and mailing addresses on the envelopes.

## Homemade Ornaments

If the glass balls and novelty characters on sale in stores seem unappealing as adornments for your tree, then create your own with the easy instructions provided here.

One of my oldest Christmas memories is making ornaments at my paternal grandmother's house. All the kids, with the help of our moms, made simple ornaments by pinning sequins onto plastic foam and satin balls. You can do this with your family, too. Buy the balls, sequins, and pins at any discount department store or craft shop. Then try your hand at creating your ornaments: Arrange different-colored sequins in a holiday shape, like a tree or star, on a red satin ball; cover an entire foam ball with a single color for a sparkling effect; or use sequins to spell out someone's name or initials on a white satin ornament.

With this project every design is an original, so you can't make mistakes. And it's great for kids as long as they're old enough to handle the pins.

❄

My sister-in-law makes "Baby's-First-Christmas" ornaments that look better than most manufactured ones. And these come with lots of love, which is unavailable in the store-bought variety. She uses a glass ball that has hung on her tree over the years, and writes out the child's name and the year he or she was born with glitter glue. Then she wraps it up and gives it to that year's special baby as a Christmas present.

❇

These unique ornaments for your tree can also be presents for a baby or married couple's first Christmas, a twenty-fifth anniversary, or for grandparents who can decorate their tree with pictures of their grandchildren.

Personalize ornaments by placing photos onto satin balls or bells. My mom liked to use our annual school portraits, but any picture will work (snapshots will need to be cut down to size). Attach the picture with glue or pins. Then create a pretty border by gluing on rickrack, pinning on sequins, or outlining the photo with glitter glue.

Or buy a cheap mini-frame and place a photo in it. Then glue on a small piece of cord or string as a hanger, and your ornament is ready for the tree.

❇

When making your gingerbread and sugar cookies, put holes at the top of a few before placing them in the oven. When they are baked, cooled, and decorated, tie a ribbon through the holes and hang them on your tree.

And the best part is that you have munchies at hand when the season comes to an end and you need to de-decorate.

❇

Save small party and wedding favors to use as ornaments. Just tie a ribbon around a little sack of almonds, a tiny basket of flowers, even a miniature parasol, and hang on the tree.

❄

Use a star cookie cutter to turn peeled apple slices into stellar shapes. Cut out the designs, and let the apple pieces dry out for a few days. Next, put a small hole in the top of each star. Thread red, green, or plaid ribbon through the holes as hangers and add to your tree.

❄

Kids can easily make their own ornaments out of felt. Here's how.

WHAT YOU NEED: Pencil; firm paper (like thin cardboard or poster board); felt; glue; gold, red, or other coordinating rickrack; a small holiday picture (such as a church, wreath, dove, or star); needle; thread; narrow ribbon to use as a hanger.

WHAT TO DO: Draw stencils of shapes for the ornaments, like a bell, Christmas tree, stocking, or snowflake on the firm paper. Cut out the stencils. With a pencil and one stencil, copy the design onto two pieces of felt and another piece of firm paper. Cut out all the shapes. Glue a piece of felt onto each side of the firm paper and let dry. Then glue rickrack around the edges of the shape as a border and let that dry. Next, glue the holiday picture to the center

## All the Trimmings

of what will be the front side of your ornament. When that's dry, make a small hole in the top of the ornament with a pin and thread a ribbon through. Tie the ribbon and your ornament is ready for hanging.

Repeat with the other stencils if you like.

❆

After you bake your holiday cookies, tie yarn or ribbons at the top of the cookie cutters and hang them on the tree as ornaments.

❆

Save pairs of mittens the kids have outgrown but that are still in good shape. Trim your tree with a few of these warm woolens by threading strong string through with a needle to make a hanger or simply attaching a wire hook directly onto the mitten.

❆

Brush clear glass balls with a thin layer of egg white. Immediately sprinkle on silver or gold glitter. Let the ornaments dry for at least 10 minutes, then place them on the tree.

❆

Hang painted pinecones on your Douglas fir this year. This is how to make them:

WHAT YOU NEED: Pinecones, floral wire (available at five-and-dime stores or craft shops), work gloves, silver spray paint, silver (or any color) glitter, a box to spray and glitter in.

WHAT TO DO: Twist a straight floral wire around one end of the pinecone, leaving a piece just long enough for hanging on the tree. With your work gloves on, spray the cone with silver paint (in the box). While the paint is still wet, sprinkle it with silver gitter, again in the box.

NOTE: This is a project best suited for adults or older children.

❆

You can help even the littlest kids make these super-easy ornaments. Cut circles and/or Christmas shapes out of poster board. Then give the kids crayons, watercolors, or markers to color in their ornaments—they can do both sides if they like. You can also pencil in designs for them to color in first, if they prefer to have guidelines.

When the decorating is done, pierce a hole at the top of each ornament and run ribbon or wire through as a hanger.

The kids can decorate an entire tree for their room with their original creations, or place them on the family tree or Grandma and Grandpa's.

## Yes, You Can Make These Decorations

With a quick trip to a discount or department store, and a little bit of time, you can make these trimmings for all the rooms in your home inexpensively and in no time flat.

Design your own tree skirt using a piece of canvas or a cotton bedsheet. Cut a circle that measures thirty inches across. Then cut a three-to-five-inch-wide hole in the center for the tree to pass through (you can also cut the skirt open so you can wrap it around the tree). With acrylic paints or fabric pens, decorate the skirt with various holiday designs. Once the paint is dry, wrap it around the base of the tree.

❄

Keep the smell of the holidays with you throughout the season. Place Christmas potpourri in various-sized glass bowls around the house for scent and decoration.

Or remove pine needles from spare tree branches and set them in baskets or bowls in several rooms to keep the smell of Christmas wafting through your whole house.

❄

Decorate plain Christmas stockings with glitter glue. We put our nicknames in the sparkly stuff. You can put your names, too, and even add holiday designs, like a Santa Claus face, snowman, or Christmas tree.

❄

Use gold paint pens and fake gems to decorate candles and candlesticks. Glue the gems onto the base of the holders (if you won't be burning the candles, you can attach some gems to them, too). Complete the design with the gold paint.

❄

Make a candy Christmas plant with the kids. Put plastic foam into a clean, empty flowerpot. Cover the sticks of clear-wrapped lollipops with green florist's tape, then stick the pops into the foam as flowers. Spread brown jelly beans over the visible foam to look like soil. And there you go—a guaranteed hit with visitors of all ages.

❄

For an inexpensive, but festive, fresh flower arrangement, fill a vase with red carnations and winter greens.

❄

Tie napkins with a red velvet ribbon and tuck a rosebud, sprig of holly, or small cinnamon stick behind the bow.

## All the Trimmings

❄

Decorate the rims of clear glass candleholders with red or green glass paint (available at craft shops or hardware stores) to give them that holiday look.

❄

Make a reusable centerpiece simply and easily by purchasing a candle wreath base from a craft or specialty shop and placing a candle in the middle.

❄

Instead of buying an expensive Christmas tablecloth that can only be used once a year, top a solid red tablecloth with a white lace one.

❄

Skip the store-bought window decorations this year and help the kids make their own. On plain pieces of paper, poster board, or cardboard, have the kids draw and cut out Christmas shapes, like Santa Claus, Christmas trees, stars, snowmen, a church, bells, etc. They can color in their designs with crayons, watercolors, poster paints, or markers.

Tape their creations to windows, the front door, even walls. The kids can also use their artwork to decorate their bedrooms or school classrooms.

❄

To replace the store-bought tinsel garland you usually string across the tree, have the kids make construction paper links. Cut pieces of construction paper into one- or two-inch-wide strips lengthwise. Make one strip into a circle and glue or tape closed. Then put another strip through the first and make a circle. Glue or tape. Continue until you think the chain is long enough.

❅

Give your coffee table the look of a snowy day by covering it with a lightly glittered sheet of white cotton you can find easily and cheap at a discount department store. Place figurines, your manger, Christmas cards, and whatever else you like on top to create your own winter scene.

❅

If your dining room chairs have spokes as backs, weave any color tinsel garland through them as a simple added touch in that room.

❅

Trim picture and photo frames with tinsel garland to brighten up any room.

## Christmas Cards Are Decorations, Too

The most boring thing to do with the zillions of holiday greetings you receive through the mail is to throw them in a basket or stick them up on a shelf until the season ends. Their varied designs light up any room in the house. Take a look at these suggestions.

Years ago, families attached Christmas cards to door frames in their living rooms, dining rooms, even the parlor—wherever people congregated during the season. And there was something warm and inviting about being surrounded by those merry wishes for the holiday season. Visitors enjoyed looking at the cards to see who had sent them, or to find their own among the many. You can bring this same nostalgic feeling into your home.

Hang Christmas cards around the borders of your doorways, including entrances between the living room and dining room, kitchen and family room, etc. With clear tape, attach horizontal cards across the top of the door frames and vertical cards down the sides. Put the tape on the inside of each card so anyone can easily lift the cover and peek inside to find out who it's from. As the season continues, your decorations will change as you receive and add more cards.

❄

Tape cards to a blank wall or on a mirror, to form the shape of a Christmas tree, wreath, or star.

Or pick up a hanging tree form from a discount or department store designed to hold the cards.

❄

Cover the front door (or any door) with red felt and pin Christmas cards to it.

❄

Pick up a large rectangular piece of plastic foam from a craft shop or five-and-dime. Cut it in the shape of a tree and pin holiday cards to it. By Christmas Day your tree will be full.

❄

Wrap a staircase railing with greens, ribbon, or garland and hang cards from it with tape.

❄

Extend a piece of cord across a mantel, large doorway, or blank wall. Spray spare clothespins red and green, then use them to attach Christmas cards to the cord.

❄

Arrange cards creatively around the house. Display cards with religious symbolism near the manger. Winter scenes work well on a coffee table or mantel also covered with greens. Stand cards together on a silver or glass tray in the middle of the dining room table as a centerpiece. Look around for other spots where cards add the finishing touch.

❄

Place cards on the branches of your Christmas tree. This is easiest with very full trees. Remember to check that none of the cards ends up sitting on top of hot lights.

## Wrap Your Gifts in These

You can skip the store-bought wraps and possibly even the ribbons with these ideas for making your own fancy packaging.

Create edible bows for gifts with red licorice whips. Tie extra-long strands around gift boxes. Then tie a bow to the top of the present, using another string. (Gift decorations like these should be attached just before giving, to ensure freshness.)

❊

You can place an odd-sized present in a gift bag, or gather it up loosely in different colored sheets of tissue paper (two or three different colors is the best mix). Make a color-coordinated bow at the top with a piece of yarn. All done.

❊

Wrap a simple red bow around a candy cane and glue the bow to the top of your package.

❊

You and the kids can paint your own wrapping paper. Cut ordinary household sponges into holiday shapes with scissors. Dip the sponges into acrylic or poster paint and press onto sheets of plain paper. When the paint dries, the wrap is ready to use.

If sponges are in short supply, use potatoes instead. Slice a potato into half-inch thick pieces. Cut each slice into a different Christmas shape (small cookie cutters make this job easier). Dip the shapes into acrylic paint and press onto plain paper for wrapping.

❄

Save newspapers from past Christmases and use as gift wrap.

❄

Instead of wasting lots of paper by trying to wrap odd-shaped or oversized gifts, simply attach a pretty bow you make yourself or pick up in a discount store.

❄

Use plain stick-on labels from a discount office supply store as gift tags. You and the kids can color them in to make them fancier.

❄

Tie thick red yarn around a mixed bunch of holly, greens, and berries, then place on gifts (and at place settings and around the house as trimmings).

Or decorate packages with holly sprigs, small pinecones, cinnamon sticks, or unbreakable ornaments tied on with a piece of plain cord or red ribbon.

❋

In place of gift wrap or gift bags, use baskets to hold presents. Line the baskets with tissue paper, cloth napkins, or colorful kitchen towels. Add a bow only if it seems necessary.

❋

Cover plain paper with holiday stickers or lick-on stamps to create your own festive design.

Or pick up a red and/or green stamp pad and a Christmasy rubber stamp or two from a craft show or holiday store. Stamp your own decoration onto plain paper.

❋

Give the kids big sheets of paper and set of crayons, markers, watercolors, poster paints, or colored pencils and let them create wrapping paper for all the gifts.

❋

Aluminum foil, sheets of tissue paper, and even colored plastic wrap all work as inexpensive gift covers. Bows, stickers, or Christmas seal stamps add the final touch.

❄

Wrap gifts in foreign newspapers—Hebrew, Russian, and Japanese all use a non-Roman alphabet which will make the packaging even more unique. After the gifts are opened, the paper just goes into the recycling bin.

❄

Skip wrapping altogether and use predecorated boxes with their own unique designs. Recipients can use these boxes as attractive storage boxes—or reuse them next year.

❄

Tape holiday candies, like star mints and Christmas-colored kisses, to gift packages in place of bows.

## Wreaths

One of the simplest and prettiest symbols of Christmas is a wreath, whether pine, wicker, or holly. Here are easy ideas for making and decorating your own.

## All the Trimmings

Instead of throwing away the branches you trim off of the bottom of the Christmas tree, save them to make your own wreath. A craft shop, discount store, or five-and-dime will carry the circular wreath forms. These same shops should have reusable decorations such as plastic fruit and pinecones, if you want them.

Attach the greenery to the wreath, decorate (if desired) and hang inside or out. When the season ends, discard the greens and pack the wreath form and decorations away until next year.

❄

Use plaid ribbon, tinsel garland, or a cranberry-and-popcorn garland strand as trimming on a simple-but-pretty pine wreath for your front door.

❄

Attach bells to the wreath on your front door. Tie several red, green, silver, or gold jingle bells onto string or cord and attach to your wreath. Place three or four of these little bundles in your greenery and listen for the sounds of guests entering your home.

❄

Trim a fresh pine wreath with plastic apples and other fruits and berries. Add sprigs of fresh holly, too. Attach a red velvet bow and place on the front door or over a fireplace.

❄

This wreath can also be reused every year. At a craft shop or five-and-dime buy a wicker or grapevine form. Wrap a two-inch thick ribbon around it. When you have wrapped the entire frame, attach the ribbon to the back of the form with a pin. Then pin a coordinating bow to the top or bottom and you're all set. Hang the wreath on the front door or in a hallway.

❄

SPECIAL NOTE TO PET OWNERS: Some holiday plants—such as poinsettia—can be toxic to animals. When decorating, keep pet safety in mind as well as child safety! Other things to watch out for: small ornaments that can be swallowed, electrical cords that can be tripped over, and trays or bowls of snacks that can be gobbled up by inquisitive dogs and cats.

# ❄❄❄❄❄❄❄❄❄❄ 6

# *Making Recycling a Part of Your Holidays*

One of the best ways to save money during the holidays is by recycling—reusing things from one Christmas to the next. This requires some thought on your part. Before you head out to the store to buy brand-new replacements or additions, you should take stock of what you have and decide what can reappear this Christmas in its old function or as something completely different. You already recycle when you pull out the same strands of lights you place on the front bushes or around the windowframes each season. And most of the ornaments that hang on your tree hold those same spots year after year. We all like buying new trimmings, but most of us just cannot afford to replace all of our old things every year. Of course, some items have sentimental value, too, and we wouldn't want to get rid of those. And so we recycle what sits in the Christmas boxes and put them out once again.

Basically, recycling means finding new uses for old things. And this chapter is filled with hints and ideas on how to do that with more than just trimmings—try wrappings, cards, and even gifts. So don't throw away anything until you have read through these pages and learned all the wonderful things you can do with what you thought was simply garbage.

## The Other Lives of Christmas Cards

Those holiday greetings can be used for more than just spreading Christmas cheer. Take a look at these suggestions.

My in-laws save all the Christmas cards they receive and use the covers as gift tags the following year. Because the cards are all different, each package comes with its own unique label.

Cards with light backgrounds work best. Simply write the recipient's name in an appropriate space on top, and add yours near the bottom.

❆

Last year's holiday greetings can be the place cards at this year's Christmas dinner party. Save the covers and write each person's name on one. Then lay the cards down flat on your guests' plates or stand them up against goblets at each place setting.

❆

Hold on to half-empty boxes of unused Christmas cards. They can be mailed out next year. If you care that anyone might remember the card from last year, save them to use the following Christmas. Or mark that box to send to new friends or business acquaintances.

❄

Use covers of old Christmas cards as ornaments. Make a hole through the top. Thread a thin piece of ribbon or cord through the hole for the hanger.

Because these cards are unbreakable, they work well on the Christmas tree for the kids' room.

❄

Use the covers from last year's Christmas cards to mail as your own holiday postcards this year. Write your original message on the back on the left-hand side and sign it. Use a rubber stamp or stickers if you want to decorate the cards. Then put the mailing address on the right, add a postcard stamp, and drop in the box.

❄

During the Christmas break, when the kids are bored, give them a set of paints or coloring pens and let them copy the designs that appear on the Christmas cards you received. For budding artists, this is an inexpensive lesson in how to draw winter scenes, faces, animals, etc. Younger children can use tracing paper to recreate their favorite images. Who knows, the kids might pick up enough ideas to create their own cards next year.

✱

Use Christmas cards in place of wrapping paper on bulky packages. Tape or glue the covers of last year's batch to the box—either cover it completely or just place them in selected spots. The kids might like this project, too. Let them attach the cards in any pattern they like.

✱

Each year the pictures on a few of the Christmas cards we receive seem too good to throw away. If you receive some of those same breathtaking images, frame the one or two you like most. Any that are clearly holiday themes can be packed away with the Christmas decorations and brought out each year in time for the holiday. But a pretty winter scene can find a spot almost anywhere in the house all year long.

## A New Look for Old Trimmings

Some decorations should not be replaced with new ones. Like these.

Instead of buying boxes of new ornaments, borrow some of your favorites from relatives who no longer use them. An elderly aunt, who will be excited that someone will be using her treasured balls again, might even suggest you keep whichever ornaments you take with you.

## Making Recycling a Part of Your Holidays

❄

Ask your parents if their Christmas boxes contain any ornaments that might be considered yours. When my husband and I got married, we each received a box of ornaments from our folks just in time for the holiday. They included special balls we had given each other when we were in college, as well as ones our parents and siblings had either made or bought for us when we were very young. These are still the ornaments we talk about most as we decorate.

❄

Save items you receive in gift baskets throughout the year to make ornaments or decorate gifts. These can include figurines, bows, pieces of fabric, and even sample-size jars of jelly.

❄

Hang popcorn-and-cranberry strands outside for birds to eat when the season is over.

Throw out stale nuts from fruit baskets to the squirrels.

The dried-apple ornaments you made for the tree this year will be munched up in no time by your backyard feathered and furry friends.

❄

When de-decorating the tree and outdoors, pack Christmas lights carefully so you can reuse them next year. If you possess the special skills required to return them to the box as they were originally packed, then certainly do so. For the rest of us lacking this ability, gently wind up each strand in itself or around a piece of cardboard and pack in a box designated only for lights. Placing tissue paper or newspaper between the strands will help prevent breakage, too. Put them in a covered box to prevent the wires from drying out. Be sure to keep this box on or near the top of the pile, where it won't be crushed by the holiday china.

❇

Instead of buying garland, use old pieces of fabric and extra ribbons to make bows. Place in your own pattern on various branches. If you pack them carefully, you can reuse them next year after a light touch-up with a steam iron.

❇

Don't discard old kids' socks or mittens, especially ones missing their mates. Try filling them with potpourri and tying closed with a ribbon. You can hang them as decorations from the fireplace, place in a wicker basket to scent the house, or put them on the tree as ornaments.

❇

If your fresh wreath came decorated this year, pull off the bow and plastic apples, berries, pinecones,

## Making Recycling a Part of Your Holidays

and holly when you take it down. Next year, pick up a less expensive plain wreath and trim it yourself with the artificial fruit and greens you saved.

❄

Before you junk any of those decorations you know will never adorn your tree, door, window, or mantel again, see if anyone you know can use what is still in good shape. Maybe a friend told you she would take that fabric tree centerpiece when you grew tired of it. Or your mom comments every year on how she must get a set of candlesticks just like yours. No reason to leave them collecting dust in the attic or, worse yet, put them in a garbage pail if new homes are waiting. Go ahead, pass them on.

❄

You like to change the way you decorate your house for Christmas each year, but it costs so much to replace your trimmings. This year pull together the remnants of your various themes from Christmases past and create something totally original.

❄

Use spare pieces of tinsel garland to wrap the bases of candlesticks, centerpieces, or even the tree. Use extra strands across a mantel, down a staircase, or in a window.

❄

Try swapping some of your indoor and outdoor decorations. If you normally put the small, twinkly lights outside and the larger screw-in bulbs on the tree inside, reverse it this year (as long as the lights are the indoor/outdoor variety). Or hang the artificial wreath you usually place above the fireplace on the outside of the house, on a window or at one of the roof peaks with some lights and a big red bow. Look around to see what else you can change this time around.

❄

Create unique centerpieces by combining spare candles, extra ornaments, a small wreath, and even leftover bows and garland. Use whatever artistic skills you have to make an attractive, yet original, table decoration.

❄

This year don't repack the ornaments that couldn't find a spot on your tree. Hang them from a chandelier, a strand of garland across a wall, a wreath, or a staircase.

## Save That Wrapping Paper

Here's how you can avoid buying lots of expensive wrapping paper, ribbons, and bows each year.

Hold on to the bows, untorn wrapping paper (remember, open those packages gently), gift boxes, and ribbons from presents you receive this year. You can use them to pack and decorate gifts you give next year.

❄

Instead of store-bought wrap, use old newspapers, spare pieces of shelf paper, out-of-date maps, or leftover pieces of fabric to cover your gifts.

❄

Save junk mail papers from home and work to wrap small gifts. If one side is blank, add stickers or draw holiday pictures for an original design.

❄

Make a new bow from snippets of ribbon. Lay several short pieces together, tie them in the middle with another piece of ribbon, and knot. Trim the ends on angles and spread out the ribbons to make a bow.

❄

Design your own wrapping paper for small gifts by gluing pictures from magazines, newspapers, and junk mail onto 11 X 17 paper. Have the kids make their own creations. Who knows, some of this wrapping paper may end up recycled by grandparents who will save it as a sample of their grandchildren's artwork.

You can also try photocopying one sheet's design

and making multiple copies of it. If you don't have access to a color copier, let the kids color in the black-and-white copies with crayons. You can also decorate some of it yourself with paints or markers.

❄

Pick up old books of wallpaper remnants from decorator stores for free (or very cheap) and use as wrapping paper.

❄

Instead of raking and throwing away all of autumn's fallen leaves, paint or glue them onto packages in place of bows or ribbons. Skip the wrapping paper altogether on plain boxes, and create a pretty arrangement with a touch of nature.

❄

Use aluminum foil (an easily recyclable product) as wrapping paper. Decorate it with removable (and reusable) bows and ribbons.

❄

A stained linen tablecloth doesn't have to hit the garbage. Cut out the unremovable spot and use it as a cleaning rag. Then use the remaining piece for gift wrapping. Tie packages with spare pieces of decorative ribbon to finish it off.

## Making Recycling a Part of Your Holidays 127

❄

Hold on to those hard-to-recycle magazines. Tear out the pages of outdated issues and use them to wrap your packages. Tape several pages together to cover larger gifts.

❄

Use finished pages from the kids' coloring books to wrap presents for grandparents and other folks on your list who will appreciate the art samples. You can glue or tape individual sheets all over the boxes, or attach a few pages together and seal up the present inside.

❄

Turn pieces of old bedsheets into gift wrap. The kids can decorate the plain ones with markers and acrylic paints.

### New Ideas on Gift Packaging

Not every gift must come wrapped in a box with lots of tissue paper.

Keep all the gift boxes you receive your Christmas presents in this year. Then next year you can say "No" each time a store clerk asks if you need a box for your purchases, because you'll have plenty at home to pack all your gifts in.

❄

Save the cookie tins you receive this year, and fill them with your own treats next year.

❄

Use mini paper bags as gift bags. Attach ribbon with glue or tape at the top to make handles. To make the bags look appropriate for the season, create holiday designs on each using stencils, stickers, crayons, markers, and/or poster paints. The kids will volunteer to help.

❄

No one really wants to buy new containers for their homemade cookies and fudge, but what can you do with all of the tins sitting in your attic with their anything-but-Christmas designs? Try redecorating them for the season by covering with spray paint, fabric, pictures, or ribbons in Christmas patterns. The unique design on each tin personalizes your gift, too.

And maybe next year some of them will be returned to you filled with more holiday goodies to munch on.

❄

Instead of wrapping gifts in the standard boxes and paper, place them in reusable baskets, brass containers, sacks, Christmas stockings, or decorative jars.

## Making Recycling a Part of Your Holidays

❄

Use empty wrapping paper and paper towel tubes as gift containers for necklaces, scarves, posters, etc. The kids can color or paint them, or glue magazine pictures to them. Or cover the tube yourself in white paper (or white spray paint), then wrap narrow red ribbon around it to look like a candy cane (the kids might like to color on the stripes with red crayons or markers instead).

❄

To package up gifts of food, fill baskets, old tins, or small wood crates you have around the house with presents and decorate them simply with ribbons.

❄

Reuse the gift bags you received last Christmas, and fill them with presents of your own for special folks on your list this year.

❄

Save strong, firm boxes from toys, small appliances, shoes, etc. to use when mailing Christmas gifts. Cross out any legible addresses and product names. Tape a piece of plain paper or an envelope on the top side to use as a mailing label. See, no brown paper necessary.

Store those polystyrene foam peanuts and shells you receive in packages in a big bag, and reuse them when putting together delicate presents or gifts to be mailed.

You can also use old newspaper to protect breakables when packaging them.

❄

If you'll be trying your hand at canning any fruits and vegetables for gift-giving this year, check around your house for spare mason jars before heading to the store to buy new ones. Ask friends and relatives for their empty containers, as well.

❄

Save tissue paper that comes in your gift boxes to reuse for the presents you hand out. Of course, only keep the pieces that are still intact.

❄

Place presents in reusable containers—you can even purchase them new and make them a part of your gifts. This is a good idea with jewelry, food, toiletries, and toys. My son's godmother brought his first-Christmas presents in a plastic tub to be used as his toy box, which came in very handy.

❄

# Making Recycling a Part of Your Holidays

Package several gifts for one person in a single box, if possible. This way you avoid purchasing extra boxes, wrap, and bows.

## Christmas Trees

Even for those of us who prefer the fresh variety of Douglas fir and blue spruce, recycling is possible.

If you can afford it, buy a live tree that can be replanted when the season ends. Though more costly than the straight fresh-cut variety, there is no waste and the extra money pays for the nice addition to your backyard landscape.

❊

Place tree branches at the base of spring-blooming bushes, such as camelias, azaleas, and rosebushes, to protect them from winter weather.

❊

Instead of depositing your tree on the curb on the specified pickup day, or finding a way to haul it down to the local dump, borrow a chipper from a friend or neighborhood landscaper and make ground cover for your trees, plants, and bushes. You can check with your local parks department to see if they have a day when they will be setting up a chipper for residents to use, too.

❊

When buying a tree stand, choose one that fits both large and small trunks so you never need another one.

❄

No reason to put the extra greens from your tree into the trash bin. The spare branches look beautiful placed across a mantel, as part of a centerpiece, or as decorative finish around a coffee table.

Or use them outside to trim the front of your house—around the doorway, for example. Add lights to complete the effect.

If you still end up with a few pieces left over after you trim the house, share them with friends and neighbors who have artificial trees and would love to bring the smell of fresh pine into their homes. The kids can stick a branch or two into the ground outside and hang small homemade bird feeders on them.

❄

When the season ends, place your tree outside with the popcorn-and-cranberry garland still on it for the birds to eat.

Or place the tree upright and hang bird feeders on it until spring.

## And Some Gift Ideas

Many of the best presents cannot be bought brand-new from a department store, at least not this year.

Look for gifts at tag sales and craft shows. Not only are they less expensive, they are almost guaranteed originals. Many crafters make their products out of recycled materials, including metals, paper, and fabric. We have a slate "Welcome" sign on our front door that's made from the shingle off of a New England Revolutionary War home.

And only at a tag sale will you find that much needed 9-iron to finish off a golf club set, or a good, but inexpensive, pair of hockey skates, size 8.

❄

Before discarding your magazines, go through them and cut out pictures you can decorate a box with. Glue the magazine pictures onto the wooden box. Let dry. Then varnish the box with clear sealer and either give it as a gift or fill it with one.

❄

Recycle gift *ideas*. If someone gives you a present for your birthday or anniversary that you know they would also like for themselves, then give him or her something similar for a Christmas gift this year.

Or take a good look around your house for favorite presents you received over the years. Someone on your list might appreciate the same thing.

❄

Put together pictures from a favorite vacation you spent with friends. Arrange the photographs in a collage frame and give as a Christmas present to your fellow vacationers.

❋

I never like going through the trouble of returning gifts I already have or just don't like. I keep more than I should in the attic and basement. If you do the same thing, then this year consider giving some of those unused wedding, shower, birthday, and anniversary presents as Christmas gifts. Just make sure your recipient is not the original giver—that would be too embarrassing!

❋

Buying for teenagers and grown children gets especially difficult. But if you've been holding on to your grandfather's pocket watch to pass on to your grandson, or your almost antique ruby ring for your daughter, give it this year as a present. So much more love comes with these gifts than something you pick out in a store. And you get the satisfaction of watching them enjoy the family heirlooms over the years.

❋

Wrap up an old ballet costume, Louisville Slugger baseball bat, a pair of tap shoes, baseball cards, even a hockey stick that is still in good condition for young children who can use this as they venture into a new sport or hobby.

## Making Recycling a Part of Your Holidays

❄

If you know how to make a patchwork quilt, or if you have the time to learn, gather up leftover pieces of fabric from relatives and friends and get sewing to make an inexpensive, but much appreciated Christmas present for practically anyone on your list.

❄

Take a close look at current fashions. Your old clothes may be in style again. If they are, but you have no desire to wear them now, pass on things in good shape as gifts to teenagers and college students who are anxious to stay on the cutting edge and will appreciate the vintage wear.

Some hand-me-downs will always be appreciated, like old army and bomber jackets, letter sweaters, sports team gear, and college sweatshirts. Check to see what's hanging in your closet or stored in your attic.

❄

Create a scrapbook of the year's events for one of your kids or grandchildren. Clip articles from magazines and newspapers that highlight the events of their first year of life. An empty photo album works even better than a real scrapbook for this present.

❄

Refill a gift basket you received with fruit, flowers, or gardening supplies.

❄

Turn some of that sports memorabilia you have lying around the house into gifts for some of the younger folks on your list who can appreciate a Brooklyn Dodgers banner, a Baltimore Colts jersey, or an autographed baseball.

❄

For new parents, used baby clothes that are like new can make a great gift. If your children wore an outfit only once or twice, why not pass it on for additional wear?

❄

If your vase collection has grown larger than necessary from fresh flowers you've received over the years, pass on a few you don't use by filling them with a holiday selection of flowers. Ask your florist for some ideas for the particular vases.

# MERRY CHRISTMAS!

❄